Betty Crocker's

Bisquick®

COOKBOOK

Betty Crocker's Bisquick® COOKBOOK

IDG Books Worldwide
An International Data Group Company
Foster City, CA • Chicago, IL • Indianapolis, IN • New York, NY

IDG Books Worldwide, Inc.
An International Data Group Company
919 E. Hillsdale Boulevard
Suite 400
Foster City, CA 94404

For general information on IDG Books Worldwide's books in the U.S., please call our Consumer Customer Service department at 800-762-2974. For reseller information, including discounts and premium sales, please call our Reseller Customer Service department at 800-434-3422.

ISBN: 0-7645-6156-1
Cataloging-in-Publication Data is available upon request from the Library of Congress.

General Mills, Inc.

Betty Crocker Kitchens
Manager, Publishing: Lois L. Tlusty
Editor: Kelly Kilen
Recipe Development: Betty Crocker Kitchens
Food Stylists: Sue Finley, Carol Grones, Mary H. Johnson

Photographic Services
Photographer: Valerie J. Bourassa, Steven B. Olson
Photography Art Director: Brett Bentrott

Cover and Book Design by Michele Laseau

CHECK OUT THE BETTY CROCKER WEB SITE: www.bettycrocker.com

Manufactured in China

10 9 8 7 6 5 4 3 2

First Edition

Cover photo: Quick Fruit Cobbler (page 200)

Dear Friends,

If you're like me, your kitchen cupboard just wouldn't be complete without a box of Bisquick on the shelf. Whether it's Saturday morning pancakes with dad or warm and yummy cobbler after the big game—you can count on Bisquick for delicious and easy recipes you know your family will love.

To celebrate seventy great years of cooking and baking with Bisquick, we've collected all of your treasured recipes—the ones you've cut off the Bisquick box or clipped from an ad—along with some soon-to-be favorites and packaged them up in this recipe scrapbook. Browse through the chapters of recipes and photos to find your favorite, or check out the All-Time FAVORITE symbol for our top consumer picks. Flip through the pages and take a nostalgic peek at Bisquick history. Learn all the essentials for the Bisquick basics, including waffles, biscuits, dumplings and more. Discover lots of ideas and helpful hints under *Betty's Tip* to make your Bisquick recipes the very best they can be.

So grab that box of Bisquick off the shelf, and let's make some memories with Bisquick today!

table of

contents

Seven Decades of Great Taste from Bisquick

Ever wonder how Bisquick, that famous "world of baking in a box," got its start? From its introduction in 1931 to the present day, Bisquick has been making great biscuits, pancakes and a whole lot more for almost 70 years. Here's a snapshot of its delicious history.

1930S: Bisquick Beginnings

In 1930, the idea for Bisquick was "born" on a train when Carl Smith, former circus promoter turned sales executive for General Mills, ordered biscuits with his meal. Though well past lunchtime, fresh, piping-hot biscuits arrived within minutes. The chef's timesaving secret? He had blended lard, flour, baking powder and salt in advance and stored the mixture in an ice chest. Smith immediately recognized the potential of a premixed baking mix, so he took the idea to Charlie Kress, the head chemist at General Mills, who began developing a top-secret biscuit mix.

Less than one year after Smith's diner-car discovery, Bisquick biscuit mix appeared on the market in 1931. It was a runaway hit! Competitors, anxious to jump on the Bisquick bandwagon, worked feverishly to develop comparable products. Within a year, 95 other biscuit mixes were introduced to the marketplace; by 1933, only six remained, with Bisquick remaining the proven leader.

The many faces of Bisquick:

1994

1986

1975

Since its beginning in the 1930s, Bisquick has been making history with great-tasting, time-honored recipes for tender biscuits, fluffy pancakes and

1940S and 1950S: Bisquick Makes It Easy

With America at war during the first half of the forties, families came to depend on the much-needed convenience of Bisquick. The Betty Crocker Kitchens continued to develop great-tasting recipes for every meal occasion, earning Bisquick the slogan of "a world of baking in a box."

In the fabulous fifties, the versatility of the "12-in-1 mix" was the name of the game. The most popular Bisquick recipes started appearing regularly on the friendly yellow box. Many of these recipe favorites are still printed on the Bisquick package today.

1960S: So Quick with New Bisquick

"Now a completely new Bisquick! Makes biscuits even lighter, fluffier than scratch!" was the headline of the fast-paced sixties, when *New* Bisquick was introduced. Designed to appeal to makers of southern-style biscuits, the reformulated Bisquick performed so well in test markets that it was rolled out into national distribution. Regular Bisquick was soon replaced, and the word *New* was dropped from the product name.

1970S: Bisquick Answers Your Recipe Requests

With the dawn of the seventies came an abundance of new Bisquick recipe ideas. *Betty Crocker's Bisquick Cookbook*, an updated version of a previous cookbook, was introduced in the fall of 1971 to help promote Bisquick as a multipurpose mix. The book was packed full with over 200 creative recipes for breads, main dishes and desserts, and was a raging success. By 1979, the cookbook was in its eighth printing!

1959

1937

1957

scrumptious waffles. For over seventy years, these and other mouthwatering treats have starred in countless advertisements, graced many a

1980s: A Milestone in Bisquick History

To celebrate the fiftieth anniversary of Bisquick, a special cookbook, *Betty Crocker's Creative Recipes with Bisquick*, was introduced. Hundreds of thousands of enthusiastic fans joined the Bisquick Recipe Club and received *The Bisquick Banner*, a quarterly newsletter that featured relevant articles, recipes for family meals and entertaining ideas.

Beginning in 1981, the "pie that did the impossible—formed its own crust as it baked" was heavily promoted with recipes, product advertising and booklets. The original Impossible Coconut Pie and Impossible Bacon Pie, which started as grassroots recipes that consumers shared with each other, quickly expanded to over 100 versions. Since then, these crustless pies have been renamed to Impossibly Easy Pies and they continue to be requested favorites.

1990s: Bisquick . . . What a Great Idea!

A desire to return to simplicity and use trusted favorites helped Bisquick continue to be a staple in homes across America. With the popularity of breads, pizzas and one-dish meals, Bisquick made it easy to get great-tasting, homemade meals on the table fast.

2000 and Beyond: The Best of Bisquick

Nearly seven decades later, America's first biscuit mix remains a baking classic and is as versatile as ever. Families continue to depend on Bisquick for delicious meal solutions everyone will love.

1943

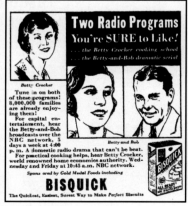
1931

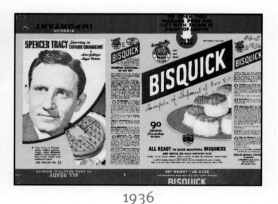
1936

product package, found themselves printed in recipe magazines and cookbooks and filled our kitchens with plenty of homemade goodness.

Quick Bisquick Tips...

※ from Betty

What's the best way to measure Bisquick?

For best results, spoon Bisquick—without sifting—into a dry-ingredient measuring cup, and level the top with a straight-edged utensil or the edge of a knife. Do not pack or tap Bisquick into the cup.

※ from Betty

What's the best way to store Bisquick?

Bisquick will keep best if stored in an airtight container or plastic bag in a cool, dry place, like on your pantry shelf. If keeping it for a longer time, store it in the refrigerator or freezer. If Bisquick is frozen, bring it to room temperature before using it.

※ from Betty

Is Bisquick affected by humidity?

Bisquick reacts to the environment just like other flour-based products do. If the weather is hot and humid, you may find that doughs and batters are more sticky, soft or wet. You can add small amounts of Bisquick to make the dough or batter easier to work with.

※ from Betty

Can I substitute Reduced Fat Bisquick for Original Bisquick in my recipes?

Sometimes you can, but because the product formulas are different the products perform differently in our recipes. The biggest difference you will find is in the amount of water that is soaked up when preparing doughs and batters. We recommend using recipes specifically written for either Original Bisquick or Reduced Fat Bisquick (like the recipes in chapter 6).

best-ever
breakfast

Autumn Brunch Waffles with Cinnamon-Cider Syrup (page 15), Frosted Cinnamon Rolls (page 14)

Frosted Cinnamon Rolls

12 rolls

2 1/2 cups Original Bisquick

2/3 cup milk

2 tablespoons sugar

2 tablespoons margarine or butter, softened

2 tablespoons sugar

1 teaspoon ground cinnamon

1/4 cup raisins, if desired

Frosting (below)

1. Heat oven to 375°. Grease rectangular pan, 13 x 9 x 2 inches. Stir Bisquick, milk and 2 tablespoons sugar until dough forms; beat 20 strokes.

2. Place dough on surface sprinkled with Bisquick; roll in Bisquick to coat. Shape into a ball; knead 10 times. Roll or pat dough into 15 x 9-inch rectangle. Spread with margarine. Mix 2 tablespoons sugar and the cinnamon; sprinkle over dough. Sprinkle raisins evenly over sugar mixture. Roll up tightly, beginning at 15-inch side. Pinch edge of dough into roll to seal. Cut into twelve 1 1/4-inch slices. Arrange with cut sides down in pan.

3. Bake 20 to 23 minutes or until golden brown. Cool slightly; remove from pan to wire rack. Cool completely, about 1 hour. Spread with Frosting.

Frosting

1 1/2 cups powdered sugar

1/4 cup margarine or butter, softened

2 tablespoons milk

1 teaspoon vanilla

Beat powdered sugar and margarine in small bowl with electric mixer on medium speed until light and fluffy. Beat in milk and vanilla until smooth and spreadable.

High Altitude (3500 to 6500 feet): Heat oven to 400°. Bake about 20 minutes.
1 Roll: Calories 240 (Calories from Fat 90); Fat 10g (Saturated 2g); Cholesterol 0mg; Sodium 440mg; Carbohydrate 35g (Dietary Fiber 0g); Protein 2g. **% Daily Value:** Vitamin A 8%; Vitamin C 0%; Calcium 6%; Iron 4%. **Diet Exchanges:** 1 Starch, 1 Fruit, 2 Fat

Betty's Tip Cutting this recipe in half is easy. Use a round pan, 8 x 1 1/2 inches, and divide the ingredient amounts in half. Roll the dough into a 9 x 7 1/2-inch rectangle, and cut into six 1 1/4-inch slices.

Autumn Brunch Waffles with Cinnamon-Cider Syrup

6 servings (Two 4-inch waffles each)

Cinnamon-Cider Syrup (below)

2 1/4 cups Original Bisquick

1 1/4 cups milk

2 tablespoons sugar

2 tablespoons vegetable oil

1 teaspoon ground cinnamon

1 egg

1/2 cup finely chopped peeled
　all-purpose apple (Braeburn,
　Gala or Haralson)

1. Make Cinnamon-Cider Syrup; keep warm. Heat waffle iron; grease if necessary.

2. Stir remaining ingredients except apple in large bowl until blended. Stir in apple. Pour batter for waffle onto center of hot waffle iron. Repeat with remaining batter.

3. Bake about 5 minutes or until steaming stops. Carefully remove waffle. Serve with syrup.

Cinnamon-Cider Syrup

1 cup sugar

3 tablespoons Original Bisquick

1 teaspoon ground cinnamon

2 cups apple cider

2 tablespoons lemon juice

1/4 cup margarine or butter

Mix sugar, Bisquick and cinnamon in 2-quart saucepan. Stir in cider and lemon juice. Cook over medium heat, stirring constantly, until mixture thickens and boils. Boil and stir 1 minute; remove from heat. Stir in margarine until melted.

High Altitude (3500 to 6500 feet): No changes.
1 Serving: Calories 530 (Calories from Fat 190); Fat 21g (Saturated 5g); Cholesterol 40mg; Sodium 830mg; Carbohydrate 81g (Dietary Fiber 1g); Protein 6g. **% Daily Value:** Vitamin A 14%; Vitamin C 2%; Calcium 16%; Iron 10%. **Diet Exchanges:** 2 Starch, 3 Fruit, 4 Fat

Waffle magic from 1940—a dinner so easy, it could have come on Santa's sleigh!

All-Time **FAVORITE**

Waffles

6 servings (Two 4-inch waffles each)

2 cups Original Bisquick

1 1/3 cups milk

2 tablespoons vegetable oil

1 egg

1. Heat waffle iron; grease if necessary.

2. Stir all ingredients until blended. Pour batter for waffle onto center of hot waffle iron. Repeat with remaining batter.

3. Bake about 5 minutes or until steaming stops. Carefully remove waffle.

High Altitude (3500 to 6500 feet): No changes.
1 Serving: Calories 240 (Calories from Fat 110); Fat 12g (Saturated 2g); Cholesterol 40mg; Sodium 600mg; Carbohydrate 26g (Dietary Fiber 0g); Protein 6g. **% Daily Value:** Vitamin A 4%; Vitamin C 0%; Calcium 12%; Iron 8%. **Diet Exchanges:** 2 Starch, 2 Fat

Betty's Tip   Way too many waffles? Freeze them! Wrap cooled muffins in aluminum foil or plastic wrap and freeze them up to 1 month. Unwrap waffles and reheat them in the 350° oven for 10 minutes or pop them in the toaster until crisp.

Wow them with wonderful waffles! It's easy—here's how:

1. Don't get stuck. To prevent waffles from sticking, season the waffle iron according to the manufacturer's directions. If greasing with cooking spray, remember to spray it before heating the iron. If you have a waffle iron with a nonstick surface, you probably won't need to grease the grids before making your waffle. Starting with a clean waffle iron is also important. After each time you use it, remove all traces of baked-on batter or crumbs.

2. Measure and mix. You can mix the waffle batter right in a 4- or 8-cup glass measuring cup that has a handle and a spout, which makes for easy pouring onto the waffle iron.

3. Pour it on. How much batter to use for making waffles depends on the model of your waffle iron. Usually it's little less than a cupful, but every waffle iron is slightly different. When you pour the batter onto the waffle iron, make sure each section of the waffle grid gets covered so it is full but not overflowing. Then close the lid and wait. When the iron stops giving off steam a few minutes later, the waffle should be done. Try lifting the lid—if it resists at all, the waffle needs a little more time to cook.

4. Use a "fork lift." A fork is great tool to use when lifting the waffle from the iron. If you're making a large batch of waffles that you want to keep warm until serving time, place them in a single layer on a wire rack or paper towel-lined cookie sheet in a 350° oven for up to 20 minutes. Just make sure you don't stack warm waffles, or they'll become soggy.

✳ Why are my waffles tough and why didn't they rise?

• Too much Bisquick or not enough liquid.
• Waffle iron too cool or too hot.

✳ Why are my waffles thin and crispy?

• Too much liquid and not enough Bisquick.

Whole Wheat Waffles with Honey-Pecan Syrup

6 servings (Two 4-inch waffles each)

Honey-Pecan Syrup (below)

2 cups Original Bisquick

1/2 cup whole wheat flour

1 1/2 cups milk

2 tablespoons sugar

2 tablespoons vegetable oil

1 egg

1. Make Honey-Pecan Syrup; keep warm. Heat waffle iron; grease if necessary.

2. Stir remaining ingredients until blended. Pour batter for waffle onto center of hot waffle iron. Repeat with remaining batter.

3. Bake about 5 minutes or until steaming stops. Carefully remove waffle. Serve with syrup.

Honey-Pecan Syrup

3/4 cup honey

1/2 cup pecan halves, toasted

1/4 cup margarine or butter

Heat all ingredients in 1-quart saucepan over low heat, stirring occasionally, until margarine is melted and mixture is hot.

High Altitude (3500 to 6500 feet): No changes.
1 Serving: Calories 560 (Calories from Fat 235); Fat 26g (Saturated 5g); Cholesterol 40mg; Sodium 710mg; Carbohydrate 75g (Dietary Fiber 2g); Protein 8g. **% Daily Value:** Vitamin A 14%; Vitamin C 0%; Calcium 16%; Iron 12%. **Diet Exchanges:** 3 Starch, 2 Fruit, 4 1/2 Fat

Betty's Tip Toasted nuts give these waffles a delicious crunch. To toast nuts, bake uncovered in an ungreased shallow pan in a 350° oven about 10 minutes, stirring occasionally, until golden brown.

Whole Wheat Waffles with Honey-Pecan Syrup

Chocolate Waffles with Caramel-Banana Topping

6 servings (Two 4-inch waffles each)

Caramel-Banana Topping (below)
1 1/2 cups Original Bisquick
1 cup sugar
1/3 cup baking cocoa
3/4 cup water
2 tablespoons vegetable oil
2 eggs

1. Make Caramel-Banana Topping; keep warm. Heat waffle iron; grease if necessary.

2. Stir remaining ingredients until blended. Pour batter for waffle onto center of hot waffle iron. Repeat with remaining batter.

3. Bake about 5 minutes or until steaming stops. Carefully remove waffle. Serve with topping.

Caramel-Banana Topping

1/2 cup packed brown sugar
1/4 cup whipping (heavy) cream
1/4 cup light corn syrup
2 tablespoons margarine or butter
1 teaspoon vanilla
3 medium bananas, sliced

Mix all ingredients except bananas in 1-quart saucepan. Heat to boiling, stirring occasionally; remove from heat. Add bananas; stir gently until well coated.

High Altitude (3500 to 6500 feet): No changes.
1 Serving: Calories 560 (Calories from Fat 160); Fat 18g (Saturated 7g); Cholesterol 90mg; Sodium 500mg; Carbohydrate 97g (Dietary Fiber 3g); Protein 6g. **% Daily Value:** Vitamin A 8%; Vitamin C 4%; Calcium 8%; Iron 12%. **Diet Exchanges:** 2 Starch, 4 Fruit, 3 1/2 Fat

Betty's Tip   These warm and wonderful waffles are not just for breakfast. For a truly decadent dessert, try these scrumptious squares topped with a scoop of vanilla or chocolate chip ice cream.

Chocolate Waffles with Caramel-Banana Topping

Belgian Waffles with Berry Cream

6 servings (Two 4-inch waffles each)

Berry Cream (below)

2 cups Original Bisquick

1 1/3 cups milk

2 tablespoons vegetable oil

1 egg

1. Make Berry Cream. Heat Belgian waffle iron; grease if necessary.

2. Stir remaining ingredients until blended. Pour batter for waffle onto center of hot waffle iron. Repeat with remaining battter.

3. Bake 3 to 5 minutes or until steaming stops. Carefully remove waffle. Top with Berry Cream.

Berry Cream

1 cup whipping (heavy) cream

1/4 cup powdered sugar

2 cups sliced strawberries

1/2 cup blueberries

Beat whipping cream and powdered sugar in chilled large bowl with electric mixer on high speed until stiff. Fold in strawberries and blueberries.

High Altitude (3500 to 6500 feet): No changes.
1 Serving: Calories 400 (Calories from Fat 225); Fat 25g (Saturated 11g); Cholesterol 85mg; Sodium 6200mg; Carbohydrate 39g (Dietary Fiber 2g); Protein 7g. **% Daily Value:** Vitamin A 14%; Vitamin C 56%; Calcium 18%; Iron 8%. **Diet Exchanges:** 2 Starch, 1 1/2 Fruit, 4 1/2 Fat

Betty's Tip   Entertaining a crowd? Try a topping bar, with choices such as sliced fruit, jam, syrup, chopped nuts, whipped cream and flavored yogurt.

Belgian Waffles with Berry Cream

All-Time
FAVORITE

Pancakes

5 servings (Three 4-inch pancakes each)

2 cups Original Bisquick

1 cup milk

2 eggs

1. Heat griddle or skillet; grease if necessary.
2. Stir all ingredients until blended. Pour batter by a little less than 1/4 cupfuls onto hot griddle.
3. Cook until edges are dry. Turn; cook until golden brown.

High Altitude (3500 to 6500 feet): No changes—except for Ultimate Melt-in-Your-Mouth Pancakes, use 1 teaspoon baking powder.
1 Serving: Calories 240 (Calories from Fat 90); Fat 10g (Saturated 3g); Cholesterol 90mg; Sodium 730mg; Carbohydrate 32g (Dietary Fiber 1g); Protein 7g. **% Daily Value:** Vitamin A 4%; Vitamin C 0%; Calcium 14%; Iron 10**%. Diet Exchanges:** 2 Starch, 2 Fat

Blueberry Pancakes: Fold 1 cup fresh or frozen (thawed and drained) blueberries into batter.

Ultimate Melt-in-Your-Mouth Pancakes: Stir 1 tablespoon sugar, 2 tablespoons lemon juice and 2 teaspoons baking powder into batter.

Fluffy pancakes are a perfect way to start a morning. Here are some pancake pointers to get you on your way:

1. Turn on the heat. Heat your skillet over medium-high heat, or turn on your griddle to 375° about 5 minutes before using. Grease the surface with a light coating of vegetable oil. If greasing with cooking spray, spray it before heating. If the surface is well seasoned or is nonstick, you may not have to grease it. To test the temperature of your skillet or griddle, sprinkle it with a few drops of water. If the water bubbles skitter around before they disappear, the heat is just right.

2. Stir it up. Stir the batter with a wire whisk or a fork, just until the ingredients are moistened. Don't worry if there are small lumps in the batter. These lumps will disappear during cooking. At this point, you can cover and refrigerate the batter for up to an hour, but don't refrigerate it longer or the pancakes may not be nice and puffy.

3. Take a test run. Start with one test pancake so you can see how your pancake batter will act. If the batter is too thin, it will spread unevenly and result in flat pancakes; a too-thick batter won't spread much at all. If you like your pancakes a bit on the thinner side, add a little milk until the batter reaches the desired consistency. For well-rounded pancakes about 4 inches wide, pour the batter onto the hot skillet or griddle using either a 1/4-cup measuring cup, a large spring-handled ice cream scoop or a large spoon.

4. Flip 'em only once! Repeated cooking on both sides will toughen rather than brown the pancakes. Flip the pancakes when they're puffed, covered with bubbles and dry around the edges. Cook the other sides until golden brown, remembering that the second side never browns as evenly as the first.

5. Keep 'em warm. If you're feeding a crowd, you can keep the pancakes warm by placing them in a single layer on a wire rack or paper towel-lined cookie sheet in a 200° oven. Be careful not to stack warm pancakes, or they'll become limp and soggy.

* *Why are my pancakes tough and leathery?*
• Griddle or skillet temperature too low or too high.
• Pancakes turned more than once.

* *Why don't my pancakes rise and get puffy?*
• Not enough Bisquick or too much liquid.
• Batter stood too long either at room temperature or in the refrigerator.
• Bisquick stored too long.
• Griddle or skillet temperature too low or too high.

Gingerbread Pancakes

6 servings (Three 4-inch pancakes each)

2 1/2 cups Original Bisquick

3/4 cup apple butter

1 cup milk

2 tablespoons vegetable oil

1/4 teaspoon ground cinnamon

1/4 teaspoon ground ginger

1/4 teaspoon ground nutmeg

2 eggs

1. Heat griddle or skillet; grease if necessary.

2. Stir all ingredients until blended. Pour batter by a little less than 1/4 cupfuls onto hot griddle.

3. Cook until edges are dry. Turn; cook until golden brown.

High Altitude (3500 to 6500 feet): No changes.
1 Serving: Calories 350 (Calories from fat 125); Fat 14g (Saturated 3g); Cholesterol 75mg; Sodium 750mg; Carbohydrate 51g (Dietary Fiber 2g); Protein 7g. **% Daily Value:** Vitamin A 4%; Vitamin C 2%; Calcium 14%; Iron 10%. **Diet Exchanges:** 2 Starch, 1 Fruit, 1 Fat

Betty's Tip Leftovers? Stack cooled pancakes between sheets of waxed paper. Wrap in aluminum foil and freeze. To reheat, unwrap pancakes and remove waxed paper. Heat on ungreased cookie sheet in 400° oven 5 to 7 minutes or until hot, or microwave uncovered on high until hot.

From 1974—self-directed pancakes, the easy way, with Bisquick.

Gingerbread Pancakes

Puffy Pancake

8 servings

2/3 cup water

1/4 cup margarine or butter

1 cup Original Bisquick

4 eggs

1 can (21 ounces) fruit pie filling
  (any flavor)

Powdered sugar, if desired

1. Heat oven to 400°. Generously grease rectangular baking dish or pan, 13 x 9 x 2 inches.

2. Heat water and margarine to boiling in 2-quart saucepan. Add Bisquick all at once. Stir vigorously over low heat about 1 minute or until mixture forms a ball; remove from heat. Beat in eggs, two at a time, beating with spoon after each addition until smooth and glossy. Spread in pan (do not spread up sides).

3. Bake 30 to 35 minutes or until puffed and edges are golden brown. Spread pie filling over pancake. Sprinkle with powdered sugar. Serve immediately.

High Altitude (3500 to 6500 feet): Not Recommended.
1 Serving: Calories 210 (Calories from Fat 90); Fat 10g (Saturated 2g); Cholesterol 105mg; Sodium 320mg; Carbohydrate 27g (Dietary Fiber 1g); Protein 4g. **% Daily Value:** Vitamin A 10%; Vitamin C 2%; Calcium 4%; Iron 4%. **Diet Exchanges:** 1 Starch, 1 Fruit, 1 1/2 Fat

Betty's Tip   All out of pie filling? Spoon cut-up fresh fruit or berries onto the pancake, and serve with vanilla yogurt or sweetened whipped cream.

Puffy Pancake

Lemon-Blueberry Wraps

6 servings (2 wraps each)

1 cup Original Bisquick

1/2 cup milk

1 tablespoon sugar

1 teaspoon grated lemon peel

2 tablespoons lemon juice

1 egg

Lemon Cream Filling (below)

About 3/4 cup fresh blueberries

1. Heat griddle or skillet; grease if necessary.
2. Stir all ingredients except Lemon Cream Filling and blueberries until blended. For each wrap, pour 2 tablespoons batter onto hot griddle, spreading each to make about 6-inch circle. Cook until tops are slightly dry. Turn and cook until bottoms are golden brown; cool.
3. Make Lemon Cream Filling. Spread about 2 tablespoons filling onto center of each wrap. Sprinkle with about 1 tablespoon blueberries; roll up.

Lemon Cream Filling

1 package (3 ounces) cream cheese, softened

1/4 cup sugar

2 teaspoons grated lemon peel

1/3 cup whipping (heavy) cream

Beat cream cheese in large bowl with electric mixer on high speed until fluffy. Stir in sugar and lemon peel; set aside. Beat whipping cream in chilled small bowl with electric mixer on high speed until stiff. Fold whipped cream into cream cheese mixture.

High Altitude (3500 to 6500 feet): Use 3/4 cup milk.
1 Serving: Calories 240 (Calories from Fat 115); Fat 13g (Saturated 7g); Cholesterol 65mg; Sodium 350mg; Carbohydrate 27g (Dietary Fiber 1g); Protein 5g. **% Daily Value:** Vitamin A 10%; Vitamin C 4%; Calcium 8%; Iron 4%. **Diet Exchanges:** 1 Starch, 1 Fruit, 1 Fat

Betty's Tip   For a pretty presentation, tie each wrap with a strip of lemon peel. Use a citrus stripper or a small knife to cut the peel.

Lemon-Blueberry Wraps

Potato Pancakes with Chunky Gingered Applesauce

6 servings (Three 4-inch pancakes each)

Chunky Gingered Applesauce
(below)

1/2 cup Original Bisquick

1/2 cup milk

1 teaspoon salt

3 eggs

3 cups finely shredded uncooked
potatoes

1. Make Chunky Gingered Applesauce. Heat griddle or skillet; grease if necessary.

2. Stir Bisquick, milk, salt and eggs in large bowl until blended. Stir in potatoes. Pour batter by a little less than 1/4 cupfuls onto hot griddle, spreading each slightly to make 4-inch pancake.

3. Cook until edges are dry. Turn; cook until golden brown. Serve with applesauce.

Chunky Gingered Applesauce

4 medium cooking apples (Rome Beauty, Golden Delicious or Greening), coarsely chopped (4 cups)

1/2 cup water

1/4 cup finely chopped crystallized ginger

1 tablespoon packed brown sugar

1/4 teaspoon ground cinnamon

Mix all ingredients except cinnamon in 2-quart saucepan. Cover and heat to boiling; reduce heat. Simmer covered 10 to 15 minutes, stirring occasionally, until apples are tender. Drain off any excess liquid. Stir cinnamon into applesauce. Serve warm or cold.

High Altitude (3500 to 6500 feet): No changes.
1 Serving: Calories 210 (Calories from Fat 45); Fat 5g (Saturated 1g); Cholesterol 105mg; Sodium 580mg; Carbohydrate g (Dietary Fiber 4g); Protein 6g. **% Daily Value:** Vitamin A 4%; Vitamin C 8%; Calcium 6%; Iron 6%. **Diet Exchanges:** 2 Starch, 1 1/2 Fruit, 1/2 Fat

Betty's Tip   Sausage links or crispy strips of bacon make a delicious accompaniment to these hearty cakes.

Potato Pancakes with Chunky Gingered Applesauce

Cardamom Rolls

10 rolls

2 1/2 cups Original Bisquick

1/3 cup milk

1 egg

2 tablespoons margarine or butter, softened

1/4 cup granulated sugar

2 teaspoons ground cardamom

1/4 cup powdered sugar

1 teaspoon warm water

1. Heat oven to 400°. Stir Bisquick, milk and egg until soft dough forms. Place dough on surface sprinkled with Bisquick; roll in Bisquick to coat. Shape into a ball; knead gently just until smooth.

2. Roll or pat dough into 10 x 8-inch rectangle. Spread with margarine. Mix granulated sugar and cardamom; sprinkle over dough. Roll up tightly, beginning at 10-inch side. Pinch edge of dough into roll to seal. Place sealed side down on ungreased cookie sheet. Cut roll at 1-inch intervals almost through to bottom, using scissors.

3. Bake about 20 minutes or until light brown. Mix powdered sugar and warm water until smooth; drizzle over warm rolls.

High Altitude (3500 to 6500 feet): Heat oven to 375°. Bake about 25 minutes.
1 Roll: Calories 185 (Calories from fat 65); Fat 7g (Saturated 2g); Cholesterol 20mg; Sodium 470mg; Carbohydrate 27g (Dietary Fiber 0g); Protein 3g. **% Daily Value:** Vitamin A 4%; Vitamin C 0%; Calcium 6%; Iron 6%. **Diet Exchanges:** 2 Starch, 1 Fat

Betty's Tip   Cardamom belongs to the ginger family and is the characteristic spice used in many Scandinavian baked goods. Although there's no true substitution, you can use 1 teaspoon ground cinnamon and 1 teaspoon ground nutmeg for the cardamom in this recipe.

Cardamom Rolls

Easy Drop Danish

12 Danishes

2 cups Original Bisquick

1/4 cup margarine or butter, softened

2 tablespoons sugar

2/3 cup milk

1/4 cup apricot preserves (or other flavor fruit preserves)

Vanilla Glaze (below)

1. Heat oven to 450°. Lightly grease cookie sheet. Stir Bisquick, margarine and sugar in medium bowl until crumbly. Stir in milk until dough forms; beat 15 strokes.

2. Drop dough by rounded tablespoonfuls about 2 inches apart onto cookie sheet. Make a shallow well in center of each with back of spoon; fill with 1 teaspoon preserves.

3. Bake 10 to 15 minutes or until golden brown. Drizzle Vanilla Glaze over warm danish.

Vanilla Glaze

3/4 cup powdered sugar

1 tablespoon warm water

1/4 teaspoon vanilla

Mix all ingredients until smooth and thin enough to drizzle.

High Altitude (3500 to 6500 feet): Heat oven to 475°. Stir 2 tablespoons all-purpose flour into Bisquick. Use 1 tablespoon sugar. Bake about 10 minutes.
1 Danish: Calories 180 (Calories from Fat 65); Fat 7g (Saturated 2g); Cholesterol 0mg; Sodium 340mg; Carbohydrate 27g (Dietary Fiber 0g); Protein 2g. **% Daily Value:** Vitamin A 6%; Vitamin C 0%; Calcium 4%; Iron 4%. **Diet Exchanges:** 1 Starch, 1 Fruit, 1 Fat

Betty's Tip   Dazzle them with **Easy Cherry-Almond Danish**. Use cherry preserves, and substitute almond extract for vanilla in the Vanilla Glaze. For an extra nutty crunch, sprinkle the glaze with toasted chopped almonds.

Easy Drop Danish

Cinnamon Streusel Coffee Cake

10 servings

Streusel Topping (below)

2 cups Original Bisquick

2/3 cup milk or water

2 tablespoons sugar

1 egg

1. Heat oven to 375°. Grease round pan, 9 x 1 1/2 inches. Make Streusel Topping; set aside.

2. Stir remaining ingredients until blended. Spread in pan. Sprinkle with topping.

3. Bake 18 to 22 minutes or until golden brown.

Streusel Topping

1/3 cup Original Bisquick

1/3 cup packed brown sugar

1/2 teaspoon ground cinnamon

2 tablespoons firm margarine or butter

Mix Bisquick, brown sugar and cinnamon. Cut in margarine, using fork or pastry blender, until mixture is crumbly.

High Altitude (3500 to 6500 feet): Heat oven to 425°. Use square pan, 9 x 9 x 2 inches. Stir 2 tablespoons all-purpose flour into the 2 cups Bisquick. Use 3/4 cup milk. Bake 15 to 20 minutes.

1 Serving: Calories 185 (Calories from Fat 65); Fat 7g (Saturated 2g); Cholesterol 20mg; Sodium 440mg; Carbohydrate 27g (Dietary Fiber 0g); Protein 3g. **% Daily Value:** Vitamin A 4%; Vitamin C 0%; Calcium 8%; Iron 6%. **Diet Exchanges:** 1 Starch, 1 Fruit, 1 Fat

1952—The country returns to normalcy and to a family classic. Why wait? It's easy to make more!

Cinnamon Streusel Coffee Cake

Cranberry-Apricot Coffee Cake

16 servings

3 cups Original Bisquick

3/4 cup sugar

1/4 cup vegetable oil

1 1/2 teaspoons almond extract

2 eggs

1 cup plain low-fat yogurt

2 cups fresh or frozen cranberries, coarsely chopped

1 cup dried apricots, coarsely chopped

1/2 cup finely chopped almonds or pecans

1/4 cup orange-flavored liqueur or orange juice

Orange-Almond Glaze (below), if desired

1. Heat oven to 350°. Generously grease and flour 12-cup bundt cake pan.

2. Stir Bisquick, sugar, oil, almond extract, eggs and yogurt in large bowl until blended. Stir in remaining ingredients except Orange-Almond Glaze. Pour into pan.

3. Bake 50 to 55 minutes or until toothpick inserted near center comes out clean. Cool 15 minutes; remove from pan to wire rack. Cool completely, about 1 hour. Drizzle with Orange-Almond Glaze.

Orange-Almond Glaze

1 cup powdered sugar

2 tablespoons orange juice

1/2 teaspoon almond extract

Mix all ingredients until smooth and thin enough to drizzle.

High Altitude (3500 to 6500 feet): Bake 60 to 65 minutes.
1 Serving: Calories 225 (Calories from Fat 90); Fat 10g (Saturated 2g); Cholesterol 25mg; Sodium 340mg; Carbohydrate 32g (Dietary Fiber 2g); Protein 4g. **% Daily Value:** Vitamin A 6%; Vitamin C 2%; Calcium 8%; Iron 8%. **Diet Exchanges:** 1 Starch, 1 Fruit, 2 Fat

Betty's Tip Sugared cranberries add a special finishing touch to this pretty coffee cake. To sugar the cranberries, roll frozen cranberries in sugar or lightly brush fresh or frozen cranberries with corn syrup, then roll in sugar.

Cranberry-Apricot Coffee Cake

Fruit Swirl Coffee Cake

18 servings

4 cups Original Bisquick

1/2 cup granulated sugar

1/4 cup margarine or butter, melted

1/2 cup milk

2 teaspoons vanilla

3 eggs

1 can (21 ounces) fruit pie filling
   (any flavor)

1 cup powdered sugar

2 tablespoons milk

1. Heat oven to 350°. Grease jelly roll pan, 15 1/2 x 10 1/2 x 1 inch or 2 square pans, 9 x 9 x 2 inches. Stir all ingredients except pie filling, powdered sugar and 2 tablespoons milk in large bowl until blended; beat vigorously 30 seconds.

2. Spread two-thirds of the batter (about 2 1/2 cups) in jelly roll pan or one-third of the batter (about 1 1/4 cups) in each square pan. Spread pie filling over batter (filling may not cover batter completely). Drop remaining batter by tablespoonfuls onto pie filling.

3. Bake 20 to 25 minutes or until golden brown. Mix powdered sugar and 2 tablespoons milk until smooth; drizzle over warm coffee cake. Serve warm or cool.

High Altitude (3500 to 6500 feet): Heat oven to 375°. Use 9-inch square pans. Use 3 1/2 cups Bisquick. Stir 1/4 cup plus 2 tablespoons all-purpose flour into Bisquick. Bake about 25 minutes.

1 Serving: Calories 220 (Calories from Fat 65); Fat 7g (Saturated 2g); Cholesterol 35mg; Sodium 430mg; Carbohydrate 37g (Dietary Fiber 1g); Protein 3g. **% Daily Value:** Vitamin A 4%; Vitamin C 0%; Calcium 6%; Iron 4%. **Diet Exchanges:** 1 Starch, 1 1/2 Fruit, 1 Fat

Betty's Tip   This easy fruit-filled coffee cake is ripe for any flavor of filling—take your pick! Try apple, cherry, blueberry, peach or apricot pie filling—or lemon curd for a luscious citrus twist.

Fruit Swirl Coffee Cake

Banana-Nut Bread

1 loaf (16 slices)

1 1/3 cups mashed very ripe
   bananas (2 large)

2/3 cup sugar

1/4 cup milk

3 tablespoons vegetable oil

1/2 teaspoon vanilla

3 eggs

2 2/3 cups Original Bisquick

1/2 cup chopped nuts

1. Heat oven to 350°. Grease bottom only of loaf pan, 9 x 5 x 3 inches.

2. Stir all ingredients except Bisquick and nuts in large bowl until blended. Stir in Bisquick and nuts. Pour into pan.

3. Bake 50 to 60 minutes or until toothpick inserted in center comes out clean; cool 10 minutes. Loosen sides of loaf from pan; remove from pan to wire rack. Cool completely, about 1 hour, before slicing.

High Altitude (3500 to 6500 feet): Heat oven to 375°. Use 1/2 cup sugar and 1/3 cup milk. Omit oil. Bake 55 to 60 minutes.

1 Slice: Calories 195 (Calories from Fat 80); Fat 9g (Saturated 2g); Cholesterol 40mg; Sodium 300mg; Carbohydrate 26g (Dietary Fiber 1g); Protein 3g. **% Daily Value:** Vitamin A 2%; Vitamin C 0%; Calcium 4%; Iron 4%. **Diet Exchanges:** 1 Starch, 1 Fruit, 1 Fat

In 1953—or any other year, people are crazy for Betty's easy, delicious bread. You'd be nuts to make it any other way!

Banana-Nut Bread

Easy Pumpkin Bread

2 loaves (8 slices each) or 1 loaf (16 slices)

1/3 cup vegetable oil

1 cup canned pumpkin

3 eggs

2 1/3 cups Original Bisquick

1 1/4 cups sugar

2 teaspoons ground cinnamon

1/2 cup raisins

1. Heat oven to 350°. Generously grease bottoms only of 2 loaf pans, 8 1/2 x 4 1/2 x 2 1/2 inches or 1 loaf pan, 9 x 5 x 3 inches.

2. Stir all ingredients except raisins in large bowl until well blended. Stir in raisins. Pour into pans.

3. Bake 8-inch loaves 40 to 50 minutes, 9-inch loaf 50 to 60 minutes, or until toothpick inserted in center comes out clean; cool 10 minutes. Loosen sides of loaves from pan; remove from pans to wire rack. Cool completely, about 1 hour, before slicing.

High Altitude (3500 to 6500 feet): Heat oven to 375°. Use 4 eggs, 2 cups baking mix and 1 cup sugar. Add 1/4 cup all-purpose flour.
1 Slice: Calories 210 (Calories from Fat 70); Fat 8g (Saturated 2g); Cholesterol 40mg; Sodium 260mg; Carbohydrate 32g (Dietary Fiber 1g); Protein 3g. **% Daily Value:** Vitamin A 34%; Vitamin C 0%; Calcium 4%; Iron 6%. **Diet Exchanges:** 1 Starch, 1 Fruit, 1 1/2 Fat

Betty's Tips For **Mini Pumpkin Breads,** generously grease bottoms only of 8 miniature loaf pans, 4 1/2 x 2 3/4 x 1 1/2 inches. Prepare recipe as directed, except bake loaves about 35 minutes.

Easy Pumpkin Bread, Cherry-Chocolate Chip Scones (page 56)

All-Time
FAVORITE

Blueberry Muffins

12 muffins

2 cups Original Bisquick

1/3 cup sugar

2/3 cup milk

2 tablespoons vegetable oil

1 egg

3/4 cup fresh or frozen (thawed and drained) blueberries

1. Heat oven to 400°. Grease bottoms only of 12 medium muffin cups, 2 1/2 x 1 1/4 inches or line with paper baking cups.

2. Stir all ingredients except blueberries in medium bowl just until moistened. Fold in blueberries. Divide batter evenly among cups.

3. Bake 13 to 18 minutes or until golden brown. Cool slightly; remove from pan to wire rack.

High Altitude (3500 to 6500 feet): Heat oven to 425°.
1 Muffin: Calories 140 (Calories from Fat 55); Fat 6g (Saturated 1g); Cholesterol 20mg; Sodium 300mg; Carbohydrate 20g (Dietary Fiber 0g); Protein 2g. **% Daily Value:** Vitamin A 0%; Vitamin C 0%; Calcium 4%; Iron 4%. **Diet Exchanges:** 1 Starch, 1/2 Fruit, 1/2 Fat

Making muffins that look and taste great doesn't involve any magic—just a few quick tips and techniques:

1. Leave the lumps. Stir the batter with a spoon just until the ingredients are moistened; the batter will look a little lumpy. If you mix the batter too much, the muffins will turn out tough and the tops will be pointed instead of nicely rounded. If you're making blueberry or other berry muffins, gently fold the berries into the batter at the very end of mixing to keep the berries from breaking apart and coloring the batter.

2. Go easy on the grease. For nicely shaped muffins with rounded tops and no overhanging edges, grease only the bottoms of the muffin cups. Better yet, use paper baking cups for easy baking and easy cleanup.

3. Divvy it up. Divide the batter evenly among the muffin cups, filling the cups about two-thirds full. Take the guesswork out of filling muffin cups: use a spring-handled ice-cream scoop! The different scoop sizes are identified by number; we recommend a No. 20 or 24. After filling the cups, be sure to wipe up any batter that spills onto the edge of the pan so it won't stick and burn. If you have empty cups in the muffin pan, fill them half full with water so the muffins bake evenly.

4. Bake and check. Bake muffins for the shortest time stated in the recipe, then check for doneness. If the muffins tops aren't golden brown or they don't spring back when touched lightly in the center, bake a minute or two longer, then check again. If the pan has a dark nonstick finish, you may need to lower the oven temperature by 25°. If you're using an insulated pan, you may need to increase the baking time slightly. Also, placing the pan on the center oven rack is important so the bottoms of the muffins don't brown too much.

5. Cool 'em on a rack. When the muffins are done, take them out of the pan immediately so they don't become soggy. Muffins baked in paper cups should lift right out. If you haven't used paper cups, loosen the muffins with a knife or metal spatula, then gently lift them out. Sometimes a recipe will tell you to leave the muffins in the pan for a few minutes before removing. This lets fragile muffins set up a bit so they don't fall apart when you take them out of the pan.

✳ *Why are my muffins peaked and full of holes?*

- Batter overmixed.
- Oven too hot.

✳ *Why don't my muffins rise?*

- Not enough Bisquick or too much liquid.
- Batter undermixed.
- Muffin cups too large.
- Entire muffin cup was greased.
- Oven too cool.
- Not baked long enough.

BEST-EVER BREAKFAST 49

Raspberry–White Chocolate Muffins

12 muffins

2 cups Original Bisquick

1/2 cup white baking chips

1/3 cup sugar

2/3 cup milk

2 tablespoons vegetable oil

1 egg

1 cup raspberries

1. Heat oven to 400°. Grease bottoms only of 12 medium muffin cups, 2 1/2 x 1 1/4 inches or line with paper baking cups.

2. Stir all ingredients except raspberries in large bowl just until moistened. Fold in raspberries. Divide batter evenly among cups.

3. Bake 15 to 18 minutes or until golden brown. Cool slightly; remove from pan to wire rack.

High Altitude (3500 to 6500 feet): Bake 16 to 19 minutes.
1 Muffin: Calories 195 (Calories from Fat 80); Fat 9g (Saturated 3g); Cholesterol 20mg; Sodium 300mg; Carbohydrate 26g (Dietary Fiber 1g); Protein 3g. **% Daily Value:** Vitamin A 2%; Vitamin C 2%; Calcium 8%; Iron 4%. **Diet Exchanges:** 1 Starch, 1 Fruit, 1 Fat

Betty's Tip For a sweet finish, dip muffin tops into melted butter and then into coarse sugar crystals or granulated sugar. Another dazzler—drizzle the tops with melted white baking chips.

It all "B"egins with Bisquick in this 1988 recipe booklet, that lets you start your day in a "B"eautiful way!

Raspberry-White Chocolate Muffins

Crumble-Topped Cranberry Muffins

12 muffins

2 tablespoons packed brown sugar

1 tablespoon Original Bisquick

1/3 cup milk

1 egg

1/2 cup whole berry cranberry sauce

2 cups Original Bisquick

2 tablespoons granulated sugar

1. Heat oven to 400°. Grease bottoms only of 12 medium muffin cups, 2 1/2 x 1 1/4 inches or line with paper baking cups. Mix brown sugar and 1 tablespoon Bisquick; set aside.

2. Stir milk, egg and cranberry sauce in medium bowl until well blended. Stir in 2 cups Bisquick and the granulated sugar just until moistened. Divide batter evenly among cups. Sprinkle with brown sugar mixture.

3. Bake about 18 minutes or until golden brown. Cool slightly; remove from pan to wire rack.

High Altitude (3500 to 6500 feet): No changes.
1 Muffin: Calories 125 (Calories from Fat 25); Fat 3g (Saturated 1g); Cholesterol 20mg; Sodium 300mg; Carbohydrate 22g (Dietary Fiber 0g); Protein 2g. **% Daily Value:** Vitamin A 0%; Vitamin C 0%; Calcium 4%; Iron 4%. **Diet Exchanges:** 1 Starch, 1/2 Fruit, 1/2 Fat

Betty's Tip For a simple twist to these easy muffins, try applesauce in place of the cranberry sauce.

Crumble-Topped Cranberry Muffins

Tropical Macaroon Scones

8 scones

2 1/2 cups Original Bisquick

1 cup diced mango

1/3 cup flaked coconut, toasted

1/4 cup sugar

1/4 cup whipping (heavy) cream

1 teaspoon vanilla

1/2 teaspoon ground nutmeg

1 egg

1 can (8 ounces) pineapple tidbits, drained

About 2 tablespoons milk

1/2 cup finely chopped macadamia nuts

About 2 tablespoons sugar

1. Heat oven to 425°. Stir all ingredients except milk, nuts and 2 tablespoons sugar until soft dough forms.

2. Drop dough by 8 spoonfuls onto cookie sheet. Brush tops with milk. Sprinkle with nuts and 2 tablespoons sugar.

3. Bake 11 to 13 minutes or until golden brown. Serve warm.

High Altitude (3500 to 6500 feet): Bake 15 to 17 minutes.
1 Scone: Calories 320 (Calories from Fat 135); Fat 15g (Saturated 5g); Cholesterol 35mg; Sodium 550mg; Carbohydrate 43g (Dietary Fiber 2g); Protein 5g. **% Daily Value:** Vitamin A 12%; Vitamin C 6%; Calcium 8%; Iron 8%. **Diet Exchanges:** 2 Starch, 1 Fruit, 2 Fat

Betty's Tip Toasted coconut adds color and crunch to these yummy scones. To toast coconut, bake uncovered in an ungreased shallow pan in a 350° oven 5 to 7 minutes, stirring occasionally, until golden brown. Or cook in an ungreased heavy skillet over medium-low heat 6 to 14 minutes, stirring frequently until browning begins, then stirring constantly until golden brown.

Tropical Macaroon Scones

Cherry–Chocolate Chip Scones

8 scones

2 cups Original Bisquick

1/3 cup finely chopped dried cherries

1/3 cup miniature semisweet chocolate chips

3 tablespoons sugar

1/3 cup whipping (heavy) cream

1 egg

About 1 tablespoon milk

About 2 tablespoons sugar

1. Heat oven to 425°. Grease cookie sheet. Mix Bisquick, cherries, chocolate chips, 3 tablespoons sugar, the whipping cream and egg until soft dough forms.

2. Place dough on surface sprinkled with Bisquick; roll in Bisquick to coat. Shape into a ball; knead 10 times. Pat dough into 8-inch circle on cookie sheet. Brush dough with milk; sprinkle with 2 tablespoons sugar. Cut into 8 wedges, but do not separate.

3. Bake 12 to 15 minutes or until golden brown. Carefully separate wedges. Serve warm.

High Altitude (3500 to 6500 feet): Heat oven to 450°. Use 2 tablespoons sugar instead of 3 tablespoons.

1 Scone: Calories 240 (Calories from Fat 90); Fat 10g (Saturated 4g); Cholesterol 35mg; Sodium 440mg; Carbohydrate 36g (Dietary Fiber 3g); Protein 4g. **% Daily Value:** Vitamin A 4%; Vitamin C 4%; Calcium 6%; Iron 6%. **Diet Exchanges:** 2 Starch, 1/2 Fruit, 1 1/2 Fat

Betty's Tip Pick your favorite fruit! Dried apricots, cranberries and blueberries make great stand-ins for the dried cherries.

Strawberry-Cream Cheese Biscuits

15 Biscuits

3 cups Original Bisquick

2 teaspoons grated orange peel

3/4 cup orange juice

1 package (3 ounces) cream cheese, softened

2 tablespoons strawberry preserves

Sugar, if desired

1. Heat oven to 450°. Stir Bisquick orange peel and orange juice until soft dough forms; beat vigorously 30 seconds.

2. Place dough on surface sprinkled with Bisquick; roll in Bisquick to coat. Shape into a ball; knead 10 times. Roll dough 1/2 inch thick. Cut with 2 1/2-inch round cutter dipped in Bisquick. Place on ungreased cookie sheet.

3. Mix cream cheese and preserves. Spoon about 1 teaspoon cream cheese mixture onto center of each dough circle. Sprinkle with sugar. Bake 8 to 10 minutes or until golden brown.

High Altitude (3500 to 6500 feet): Not Recommended.
1 Biscuit: Calories 135 (Calories from Fat 45); Fat 5g (Saturated 2g); Cholesterol 5mg; Sodium 360mg; Carbohydrate 20g (Dietary Fiber 0g); Protein 2g. **% Daily Value:** Vitamin A 2%; Vitamin C 4%; Calcium 4%; Iron 4%. **Diet Exchanges:** 1 Starch, 1 Fat

Maple Breakfast Sandwiches

6 sandwiches

2 1/3 cups Original Bisquick

1/2 cup milk

3 tablespoons maple-flavored syrup

3 tablespoons margarine or butter, melted

1 package (7 or 8 ounces) frozen sausage patties

3 slices process American cheese, cut diagonally in half

1. Heat oven to 425°. Stir Bisquick, milk, maple syrup and margarine until soft dough forms (dough will be sticky).

2. Place dough on surface sprinkled with Bisquick; roll in Bisquick to coat. Shape into a ball; knead 8 to 10 times. Roll dough 1/2 inch thick. Cut with 3-inch round cutter dipped in Bisquick. Place on ungreased cookie sheet. Bake 10 to 12 minutes or until golden brown.

3. Cook sausage patties as directed on package. Cut warm biscuits horizontally in half. Place sausage patty and piece of cheese in each biscuit. Serve with additional maple syrup if desired.

High Altitude (3500 to 6500 feet): Heat oven to 450°. Bake 9 to 11 minutes.
1 Sandwich: Calories 460 (Calories from Fat 270); Fat 30g (Saturated 10g); Cholesterol 45mg; Sodium 1230mg; Carbohydrate 37g (Dietary Fiber 1g); Protein 12g. **% Daily Value:** Vitamin A 12%; Vitamin C 0%; Calcium 18%; Iron 10%. **Diet Exchanges:** 2 Starch, 1 High-Fat Meat, 1/2 Fruit, 4 Fat

Betty's Tip Have it your way! Try slices of Canadian-style bacon or fully cooked ham instead of the sausage patties if you like.

Maple Breakfast Sandwiches

Do-Ahead Egg and Sausage Bake

6 servings

1 pound bulk pork sausage

1 cup Original Bisquick

1 cup shredded Cheddar cheese
   (4 ounces)

2 cups milk

1 teaspoon ground mustard

1/2 teaspoon dried oregano leaves

6 eggs, slightly beaten

1. Grease 2-quart casserole. Cook sausage in 10-inch skillet over medium heat, stirring occasionally, until no longer pink; drain.

2. Mix sausage and remaining ingredients. Pour into casserole. Cover and refrigerate at least 4 hours but no longer than 24 hours.

3. Heat oven to 350°. Bake uncovered about 1 hour or until knife inserted in center comes out clean.

High Altitude (3500 to 6500 feet): Use 2/3 cup Bisquick. Bake about 1 1/4 hours.
1 Serving: Calories 615 (Calories from Fat 430); Fat 48g (Saturated 20g); Cholesterol 310mg; Sodium 1230mg; Carbohydrate 7g (Dietary Fiber 0g); Protein 29g. **% Daily Value:** Vitamin A 14%; Vitamin C 0%; Calcium 28%; Iron 12%. **Diet Exchanges:** 1 Starch, 4 High-Fat Meat, 5 Fat

Betty's Tip This is a perfect make-ahead dish for a crowd. Serve with crispy hash brown potatoes and a platter of fresh fruit.

Do-Ahead Egg and Sausage Bake

Savory Apple Brunch Bake

8 servings

1 pound bacon

1 medium unpeeled cooking apple
(Rome Beauty, Golden Delicious
or Greening), peeled and
chopped (1 cup)

2 tablespoons sugar

1 1/2 cups Original Bisquick

1 1/2 cups milk

4 eggs

2 cups shredded Cheddar cheese
(8 ounces)

1. Heat oven to 375°. Grease rectangular baking dish,
   11 x 7 x 1 1/2 inches. Cook bacon in 12-inch skillet over
   medium heat, turning occasionally, until crisp; drain on
   paper towels and cool. Crumble bacon into small pieces.

2. Mix apple and sugar; spread in baking dish. Stir
   Bisquick, milk and eggs until blended; pour over apple.
   Sprinkle with bacon and cheese.

3. Bake uncovered 30 to 35 minutes or until knife inserted
   in center comes out clean.

High Altitude (3500 to 6500 feet): No changes.
1 Serving: Calories 370 (Calories from Fat 215); Fat 24g (Saturated 11g); Cholesterol
150mg; Sodium 800mg; Carbohydrate 22g (Dietary Fiber 1g); Protein 18g. **% Daily
Value:** Vitamin A 12%; Vitamin C 0%; Calcium 26%; Iron 8%. **Diet Exchanges:**
1 Starch, 2 High-Fat Meat, 1/2 Fruit, 1 1/2 Fat

Betty's Tip Brunch is a breeze when you serve this tasty dish with
crisp apple slices and mixed baby salad greens, along with a pitcher of
freshly squeezed orange juice.

Savory Apple Brunch Bake

Hawaiian Brunch Pizza

8 servings

1 1/2 cups Original Bisquick

1/3 cup very hot water

3/4 cup sour cream

1/2 teaspoon onion salt

3 eggs

1 package (6 ounces) sliced Canadian-style bacon, cut into thin strips

1 cup shredded Cheddar cheese (4 ounces)

1 can (20 ounces) pineapple chunks, well drained

1/4 cup chopped green bell pepper

1. Heat oven to 425°. Grease 12-inch pizza pan.

2. Mix Bisquick and hot water until soft dough forms. Press dough in pizza pan, using fingers dusted with Bisquick; pinch edge to form 1/2-inch rim. Bake 10 minutes.

3. Mix sour cream, onion salt and eggs; pour over crust. Layer bacon, cheese, pineapple and bell pepper on egg mixture. Bake about 25 minutes or until set. Cool slightly before serving.

High Altitude (3500 to 6500 feet): Use 1/2 cup boiling water to make dough.
1 Serving: Calories 285 (Calories from Fat 135); Fat 15g (Saturated 7g); Cholesterol 115mg; Sodium 760mg; Carbohydrate 26g (Dietary Fiber 1g); Protein 12g. **% Daily Value:** Vitamin A 8%; Vitamin C 8%; Calcium 14%; Iron 8%. **Diet Exchanges:** 1 Starch, 1 1/2 Medium-Fat Meat, 1 Fruit, 1 Fat

Betty's Tip Make this brunch pizza on the weekend, and freeze left-over individual slices to use for a quick weekday breakfast. Just thaw in the refrigerator overnight, then zap in the microwave about 1 minute or until hot.

Hawaiian Brunch Pizza

Cheesy Bacon Quiche

6 servings

1 1/4 cups Original Bisquick

1/4 cup margarine or butter, softened

2 tablespoons boiling water

1 cup shredded Swiss cheese (4 ounces)

1 package (6 ounces) sliced Canadian-style bacon, chopped

4 medium green onions, sliced (1/4 cup)

1 1/2 cups half-and-half

3 eggs

1/2 teaspoon salt

1/4 teaspoon ground red pepper (cayenne)

1. Heat oven to 400°. Grease pie plate, 9 x 1 1/4 inches. Stir Bisquick and margarine until blended. Add boiling water; stir vigorously until soft dough forms. Press dough on bottom and up side of pie plate, forming edge on rim of pie plate.

2. Sprinkle cheese, bacon and onions over crust. Beat half-and-half and eggs; stir in salt and red pepper. Pour into crust.

3. Bake 35 to 40 minutes or until knife inserted in center comes out clean. Let stand 10 minutes before serving.

High Altitude (3500 to 6500 feet): Heat oven to 375°. Bake about 40 minutes.
1 Serving: Calories 370 (Calories from Fat 235); Fat 26g (Saturated 11g); Cholesterol 145mg; Sodium 840mg; Carbohydrate 23g (Dietary Fiber 2g); Protein 13g. **% Daily Value:** Vitamin A 22%; Vitamin C 4%; Calcium 30%; Iron 8%. **Diet Exchanges:** 1 Starch, 1 High-Fat Meat, 2 Vegetable, 3 Fat

Betty's Tip For an easy-on-the-cook brunch, do as much as possible ahead of time. Chop the Canadian-style bacon, shred the cheese and slice the onions. You can even combine the half-and-half mixture. The quiche will be a snap to put together in the morning.

Cheesy Bacon Quiche, Strawberry–Cream Cheese Biscuits (page 57)

savory
snacks and

Sausage-Cheese Balls (page 77), Cheese-Garlic Biscuits (page 70), Hot 'n' Spicy Chicken Drummies (page 71)

breads

Cheese-Garlic Biscuits

9 biscuits

2 cups Original Bisquick

2/3 cup milk

1/2 cup shredded Cheddar cheese
(2 ounces)

2 tablespoons margarine or butter,
melted

1/8 teaspoon garlic powder

1. Heat oven to 450°. Stir Bisquick, milk and cheese until soft dough forms.

2. Drop dough by 9 spoonfuls onto ungreased cookie sheet.

3. Bake 8 to 10 minutes or until golden brown. Mix margarine and garlic powder; brush over warm biscuits.

High Altitude (3500 to 6500 feet): Heat oven to 475°. Bake 9 to 11 minutes.
1 Biscuit: Calories 165 (Calories from Fat 80); Fat 9g (Saturated 3g); Cholesterol 5mg; Sodium 460mg; Carbohydrate 17g (Dietary Fiber 0g); Protein 4g. **% Daily Value:** Vitamin A 6%; Vitamin C 0%; Calcium 10%; Iron 4%. **Diet Exchanges:** 1 Starch, 2 Fat

As the century draws to a close in 1999, Bisquick takes the tricks out of harried lives, and brings back the treats.

Hot 'n' Spicy Chicken Drummies

2 dozen appetizers

1 cup red pepper sauce

1 teaspoon garlic salt

24 chicken drummettes

2 tablespoons margarine or butter

1 cup Original Bisquick

3/4 teaspoon onion salt

1/2 teaspoon pepper

1/4 teaspoon ground red pepper (cayenne)

Blue cheese dressing, if desired

1. Mix pepper sauce and garlic salt. Pour over chicken in shallow glass or plastic dish. Cover and refrigerate at least 4 hours but no longer than 24 hours.

2. Heat oven to 450°. Melt margarine in jelly roll pan, 15 1/2 x 10 1/2 x 1 inch, in oven. Mix Bisquick, onion salt, pepper and red pepper. Remove chicken from sauce; discard sauce. Dip chicken in Bisquick to coat. Place in single layer in pan.

3. Bake 25 minutes; turn. Bake 20 to 25 minutes longer or until chicken is golden brown and juice is no longer pink when centers of pieces are cut. Serve with dressing.

High Altitude (3500 to 6500 feet): No changes.
1 Appetizer: Calories 115 (Calories from Fat 70); Fat 8g (Saturated 2g); Cholesterol 30mg; Sodium 220mg; Carbohydrate 2g (Dietary Fiber 0g); Protein 9g. **% Daily Value:** Vitamin A 2%; Vitamin C 2%; Calcium 0%; Iron 2%. **Diet Exchanges:** 1 Medium-Fat Meat, 1 Fat

Betty's Tip Cool down with a side of blue cheese dressing, or try drummies with a bowl of sour cream, plain yogurt, or ranch dressing. Wild about wings? Substitute 12 chicken wings (about 2 pounds) for the drummettes.

Apricot-Glazed Coconut-Chicken Bites

About 3 dozen appetizers

1/2 cup sweetened condensed milk

2 tablespoons Dijon mustard

1 1/2 cups Original Bisquick

2/3 cup flaked coconut

1/2 teaspoon salt

1/2 teaspoon paprika

1 pound boneless, skinless chicken breast halves, cut into 1-inch pieces

1/4 cup margarine or butter, melted

Apricot Glaze (below)

Hot mustard, if desired

1. Heat oven to 425°. Mix milk and Dijon mustard. Mix Bisquick, coconut, salt and paprika. Dip chicken into milk mixture, then coat with Bisquick.

2. Pour 2 tablespoons of the melted margarine in jelly roll pan, 15 1/2 x 10 1/2 x 1 inch. Place coated chicken in pan. Drizzle remaining margarine over chicken.

3. Bake uncovered 20 minutes. Make Apricot Glaze. Turn chicken; brush with glaze. Bake 10 to 15 minutes longer or until chicken is no longer pink in center and glaze is bubbly. Serve with hot mustard.

Apricot Glaze

1/2 cup apricot spreadable fruit

2 tablespoons honey

2 tablespoons Dijon mustard

1 tablespoon white vinegar

Stir all ingredients until blended.

High Altitude (3500 to 6500 feet): No changes.
1 Appetizer: Calories 80 (Calories from Fat 25); Fat 3g (Saturated 1g); Cholesterol 5mg; Sodium 160mg; Carbohydrate 10g (Dietary Fiber 0g); Protein 3g. **% Daily Value:** Vitamin A 2%; Vitamin C 0%; Calcium 2%; Iron%. **Diet Exchanges:** 1/2 Starch, 1 Fat

Betty's Tip In 1986, Coconut Chicken Breasts took first place in the Bisquick Invitational recipe contest for professional chefs and cooks. We've taken this winning combination, added a fruity twist and scaled it down to snack size—it's a winner for everyone!

Apricot-Glazed Coconut -Chicken Bites

Mini Chinese Chicken Snacks

2 dozen appetizers

1 1/4 cups Original Bisquick

1/4 cup margarine or butter, softened

2 tablespoons boiling water

1/2 cup half-and-half

1 egg

1/3 cup finely shredded carrot

1/3 cup drained sliced water chestnuts (from 8-ounce can), chopped

1 tablespoon grated lemon peel

1/2 teaspoon salt

1/2 teaspoon garlic powder

1/2 teaspoon five-spice powder

1 medium green onion, thinly sliced (1 tablespoon)

1 can (5 ounces) chunk chicken, drained

1. Heat oven to 375°. Generously grease 24 small muffin cups, 1 3/4 x 1 inch. Stir Bisquick and margarine until blended. Add boiling water; stir vigorously until soft dough forms. Press rounded teaspoonful of dough on bottom and up side of each cup.

2. Beat half-and-half and egg in medium bowl. Stir in remaining ingredients. Spoon about 1 tablespoon mixture into each cup.

3. Bake 20 to 25 minutes or until edges are golden brown and centers are set. Serve warm. Store covered in refrigerator.

High Altitude (3500 to 6500 feet): No changes.
1 Appetizer: Calories 65 (Calories from Fat 35); Fat 4g (Saturated 1g); Cholesterol 15mg; Sodium 190mg; Carbohydrate 5g (Dietary Fiber 0g); Protein 2g. **% Daily Value:** Vitamin A 6%; Vitamin C 0%; Calcium 2%; Iron 2%. **Diet Exchanges:** 1/2 Starch, 1/2 Fat

Betty's Tip Dress up these picture-perfect party bits by garnishing with shredded carrot, sliced radish, sliced green onion, chopped fresh parsley, red pepper strips or celery leaves.

Mini Cheese Chicken Snacks

Steamed Beef Dumplings

30 appetizers

Soy Dipping Sauce (below)

2 tablespoons soy sauce

1 teaspoon cornstarch

2 medium carrots, shredded (1 cup)

2 medium green onions, thinly
sliced (2 tablespoons)

2 tablespoons chopped fresh
cilantro

1/4 teaspoon salt

3/4 pound ground beef

2 cups Original Bisquick

1/4 cup boiling water

2 tablespoons cold water

1. Make Soy Dipping Sauce; set aside. Mix soy sauce and corn-starch in large bowl. Stir in carrots, onions, cilantro and salt. Add beef; mix well. Shape mixture into 30 meatballs, using about 1 tablespoon for each; set aside.

2. Stir Bisquick and boiling water in medium bowl until soft dough forms. Stir in cold water until dough forms a ball (dough will be sticky). Divide dough in half. Return one half of dough to bowl; cover and set aside. Divide other half of dough into 15 balls. Roll each ball into 3-inch circle on surface sprinkled with Bisquick. Place 1 meatball in center of each dough circle. Fold dough up and around meatball, allowing meatball to show at the top. Press dough firmly around meatball, pleating to fit. Gently flatten bottom of each dumpling. Repeat with remaining dough and meatballs.

3. Place steamer basket in 1/2 inch water in 3-quart saucepan (water should not touch bottom of basket). Place dumplings, open side up, in basket so edges don't touch. (If all dumplings won't fit in basket, refrigerate remainder until ready to steam.) Cover tightly and heat to boiling; reduce heat to low. Cover and steam dumplings 16 to 18 minutes or until beef is no longer pink in center. Remove dumplings from steamer. Press dough firmly around meatballs. Serve warm with sauce.

Soy Dipping Sauce

1/4 cup rice vinegar

1/4 cup soy sauce

1 medium green onion (1 tablespoon), thinly sliced

Mix vinegar and soy sauce. Sprinkle with onion.

High Altitude (3500 to 6500 feet): No changes.
1 Appetizer: Calories 65 (Calories from Fat 25); Fat 3g (Saturated 1g); Cholesterol 5mg; Sodium 320mg; Carbohydrate 6g (Dietary Fiber 0g); Protein 3g. **% Daily Value:** Vitamin A 6%; Vitamin C 0%; Calcium 2%; Iron 2%. **Diet Exchanges:** 1/2 Starch, 1/2 Fat

Betty's Tip If you don't have a steamer, don't despair! Place dumplings, open side up, on a greased cookie sheet. Bake 10 to 15 minutes in a 375° oven.

Sausage-Cheese Balls

About 8 1/2 dozen appetizers

3 cups Original Bisquick

1 pound uncooked bulk pork
sausage

4 cups shredded Cheddar cheese
(16 ounces)

1/2 cup grated Parmesan cheese

1/2 cup milk

1/2 teaspoon dried rosemary
leaves, crumbled

1 1/2 teaspoons chopped fresh
parsley or 1/2 teaspoon parsley
flakes

1. Heat oven to 350°. Lightly grease jelly roll pan,
   15 1/2 x 10 1/2 x 1 inch.

2. Stir all ingredients until well mixed (you may need
   to use your hands). Shape mixture into 1-inch balls.
   Place in pan.

3. Bake 20 to 25 minutes or until brown. Immediately
   remove from pan. Serve warm.

High Altitude (3500 to 6500 feet): Heat oven to 375°. Use 2 1/2 cups Bisquick.
Stir 1/2 cup all-purpose flour into Bisquick. For Holiday Ham Balls, no changes.
1 Appetizer: Calories 45 (Calories from Fat 25); Fat 3g (Saturated 1g); Cholesterol
5mg; Sodium 110mg; Carbohydrate 2g (Dietary Fiber 0g); Protein 2g **% Daily Value:**
Vitamin A 0%; Vitamin C 0%; Calcium 4%; Iron 0% **Diet Exchanges:** 1 Fat

Holiday Ham Balls: Substitute 1 1/2 cups finely chopped fully cooked
ham for the sausage. Omit rosemary. Add 2 tablespoons parsley flakes
and 2/3 cup milk. Mix and bake as directed.

Betty's Tip Get a jump start on your party with these tasty nibbles.
Make them up to a day ahead of time and refrigerate; bake as directed.
Or, cover and freeze unbaked balls up to 1 month. Bake frozen balls 25
to 30 minutes or until brown.

Sesame Pork Strips

About 3 dozen appetizers

1 tablespoon margarine or butter, melted

1 pound pork boneless loin chops, 1 inch thick

1 1/4 cups Original Bisquick

1/3 cup sesame seed

1 teaspoon salt

1 teaspoon paprika

1 teaspoon ground mustard

2 eggs

2 tablespoons milk

2 tablespoons margarine or butter, melted

Sweet-and-sour sauce or mustard, if desired

1. Heat oven to 400°. Spread 1 tablespoon melted margarine in jelly roll pan, 15 1/2 x 10 1/2 x 1 inch. Remove fat from pork. Cut pork into 1/4-inch slices; cut slices into 1/2-inch-wide strips.

2. Mix Bisquick, sesame seed, salt, paprika and mustard. Beat eggs and milk with fork. Dip pork strips into egg mixture, then coat with sesame seed mixture. Place in single layer in pan. Drizzle 2 tablespoons melted margarine over pork.

3. Bake 25 to 30 minutes or until brown and crisp. Serve with sweet-and-sour sauce.

High Altitude (3500 to 6500 feet): No changes.
1 Appetizer: Calories 50 (Calories from Fat 25); Fat 3g (Saturated 1g); Cholesterol 20mg; Sodium 115mg; Carbohydrate 2g (Dietary Fiber 0g); Protein 4g. **% Daily Value:** Vitamin A 2%; Vitamin C 0%; Calcium 0%; Iron 2%. **Diet Exchanges:** 1/2 Lean Meat, 1/2 Fat

Betty's Tip   This sesame coating is equally delicious on chicken. To make **Sesame Chicken Strips,** substitute 4 boneless, skinless chicken breast halves (about 1 1/4 pounds) for the pork.

Steamed Beef Dumplings (page 76), Sesame Pork Strips

Crab Cakes

About 2 dozen appetizers

1 tablespoon margarine or butter

1/3 cup chopped onion

1/3 cup chopped celery

1/3 cup chopped bell pepper

1 cup soft bread crumbs

1/2 cup Original Bisquick

2 teaspoons Worcestershire sauce

1/4 teaspoon pepper

1/4 teaspoon salt

2 eggs, slightly beaten

1 package (14 ounces) imitation crabmeat flakes, chopped

Cocktail sauce, if desired

1. Heat oven to 400°. Generously grease 2 cookie sheets. Melt margarine in 10-inch skillet over medium heat. Cook onion, celery and bell pepper in margarine about 3 minutes, stirring occasionally, until crisp-tender.

2. Mix vegetable mixture and remaining ingredients except cocktail sauce. Shape mixture into 1 1/2-inch patties. Place on cookie sheets.

3. Bake about 12 minutes, turning once, until golden brown. Serve with cocktail sauce.

High Altitude (3500 to 6500 feet): No changes.
1 Appetizer: Calories 60 (Calories from Fat 20); Fat 2g (Saturated 0g); Cholesterol 20mg; Sodium 260mg; Carbohydrate 6g (Dietary Fiber 0g); Protein 4g. **% Daily Value:** Vitamin A 2%; Vitamin C 2%; Calcium 2%; Iron 2%. **Diet Exchanges:** 1 Lean Meat

Betty's Tip You don't have to turn on your oven to enjoy these savory cakes—use a skillet instead. Heat 1 tablespoon vegetable oil in a 10-inch skillet over medium-high heat. Cook patties in oil 4 to 5 minutes, turning once, until golden.

Crab Cakes

Creamy Tuna Garden Wedges

About 18 appetizers

1 1/2 cups Original Bisquick

1/3 cup boiling water

2 medium green onions, sliced (2 tablespoons)

1 package (8 ounces) cream cheese, softened

1/2 cup sour cream

1 teaspoon dried dill weed

1/8 teaspoon garlic powder

1 can (6 ounces) tuna in water, drained

3 cups fresh vegetables (sliced radishes, celery or red onion; chopped broccoli, cauliflower, bell pepper or yellow summer squash)

1 cup shredded cheese (4 ounces), if desired

1. Heat oven to 450°. Stir Bisquick, boiling water and onions in medium bowl until soft dough forms; beat vigorously 20 strokes.

2. Press dough in ungreased 12-inch pizza pan, using fingers dusted with Bisquick; pinch edge to form 1/2-inch rim. Bake about 10 minutes or until light brown. Cool 10 minutes.

3. Stir cream cheese, sour cream, dill weed, garlic powder and tuna until blended; spread evenly over crust. Refrigerate 1 to 2 hours or until chilled. Just before serving, top with vegetables and cheese. Cut into wedges.

High Altitude (3500 to 6500 feet): Heat oven to 475°.
1 Appetizer: Calories 100 (Calories from Fat 45); Fat 5g (Saturated 4g); Cholesterol 20mg; Sodium 200mg; Carbohydrate 8g (Dietary Fiber 0g); Protein 4g. **% Daily Value:** Vitamin A 8%; Vitamin C 12%; Calcium 4%; Iron 4%. **Diet Exchanges:** 2 Vegetable, 1 Fat

Betty's Tip This fresh-tasting appetizer is incredibly versatile! You can leave out the tuna for a meatless treat or replace it with 1/2 to 1 cup chopped cooked crabmeat.

Creamy Tuna Garden Wedges

Pesto Appetizer Squares

4 dozen appetizers

4 cups Original Bisquick

1 cup milk

2 eggs

1/3 cup basil pesto

1/2 cup spaghetti sauce, heated

Chopped fresh basil, if desired

Grated Parmesan cheese, if desired

1. Heat oven to 375°. Grease rectangular pan, 13 x 9 x 2 inches.

2. Mix Bisquick, milk, eggs and pesto. Spread in pan.

3. Bake 25 to 30 minutes or until golden brown; cool slightly. For squares, cut into 8 rows by 6 rows. Top each square with about 1/2 teaspoon spaghetti sauce. Sprinkle with basil and cheese.

High Altitude (3500 to 6500 feet): No changes.
1 Appetizer: Calories 55 (Calories from Fat 30); Fat 3g (Saturated 1g); Cholesterol 10mg; Sodium 160mg; Carbohydrate 7g (Dietary Fiber 0g); Protein 1g. **% Daily Value:** Vitamin A 0%; Vitamin C 0%; Calcium 3%; Iron 2%. **Diet Exchanges:** 1 Starch

Who is the "Hostess with the Mostest" in this 1957 cookbook? You are, with Betty and a box of Bisquick!

Pesto Appetizer Squares

Mexican Cheese Snacks

About 4 dozen appetizers

1 1/2 cups Original Bisquick

1/4 cup sour cream

1 egg

1 can (4 ounces) chopped green
chilies, drained

1 cup shredded Cheddar cheese
(4 ounces)

1. Heat oven to 400°. Grease cookie sheet. Stir Bisquick, sour cream, egg and chilies until blended. Stir in cheese.

2. Drop dough by rounded teaspoonfuls about 2 inches apart onto cookie sheet.

3. Bake 10 to 12 minutes or until golden brown. Serve warm.

High Altitude (3500 to 6500 feet): Heat oven to 425°. Bake 8 to 10 minutes.
1 Appetizer: Calories 30 (Calories from Fat 20); Fat 2g (Saturated 1g); Cholesterol 5mg; Sodium 75mg; Carbohydrate 2g (Dietary Fiber 0g); Protein 1g. **% Daily Value:** Vitamin A 0%; Vitamin C 0%; Calcium 0%; Iron 0%. **Diet Exchanges:** 1/2 Fat

Betty's Tip These little bites are the perfect do-ahead appetizer. Spoon the dough onto a greased cookie sheet and refrigerate up to 4 hours. Pop them in the oven about 10 minutes before your guests arrive.

Mexican Cheese Snacks

String Cheese Sticks

8 cheese sticks

2 1/4 cups Original Bisquick

2/3 cup milk

1 package (8 ounces) smoked
string cheese

1 tablespoon margarine or butter,
melted

1/4 teaspoon garlic powder

1 can (8 ounces) pizza sauce,
heated

1. Heat oven to 450°. Stir Bisquick and milk until soft dough forms; beat 30 seconds. Place dough on surface sprinkled with Bisquick; gently roll in Bisquick to coat. Shape into a ball; knead 10 times.

2. Roll dough 1/4 inch thick. Cut into eight 6 x 2-inch rectangles. Roll each rectangle around 1 piece of cheese. Pinch edge into roll to seal; seal ends. Roll on surface to completely enclose cheese sticks. Place seam sides down on ungreased cookie sheet.

3. Bake 8 to 10 minutes or until golden brown. Mix margarine and garlic powder; brush over warm cheese sticks before removing from cookie sheet. Serve warm with pizza sauce for dipping.

High Altitude (3500 to 6500 feet): Bake 10 to 12 minutes.
1 Stick: Calories 255 (Calories from Fat 110); Fat 12g (Saturated 2g); Cholesterol 5mg; Sodium 810mg; Carbohydrate 25g (Dietary Fiber 1g); Protein 11g. **% Daily Value:** Vitamin A 14%; Vitamin C 6%; Calcium 30%; Iron 6%. **Diet Exchanges:** 1 1/2 Starch, 1 Medium-Fat Meat, 1 1/2 Fat

Betty's Tip If you don't have pizza sauce on hand, you can use spaghetti sauce or salsa. You can also substitute regular string cheese for the smoked string cheese.

String Cheese Sticks

Zucchini Bites

4 dozen appetizers

4 small unpeeled zucchini, thinly
    sliced (3 cups)

1 cup Original Bisquick

1 medium onion, finely chopped
    (1/2 cup)

1/2 cup grated Parmesan cheese

1/2 cup vegetable oil

2 tablespoons chopped fresh
    parsley

1/2 teaspoon salt

1/2 teaspoon seasoned salt

1/2 teaspoon dried marjoram
    or oregano leaves

1 clove garlic, finely chopped

4 eggs, slightly beaten

1. Heat oven to 350°. Grease bottom and sides of rectangular pan, 13 x 9 x 2 inches.

2. Stir all ingredients until blended. Spread in pan.

3. Bake about 25 minutes or until golden brown. Cut into 2-inch squares; cut squares diagonally in half into triangles.

High Altitude (3500 to 6500 feet): Heat oven to 375°.
1 Appetizer: Calories 40 (Calories from Fat 25); Fat 3g (Saturated 1g); Cholesterol 20mg; Sodium 95mg; Carbohydrate 2g (Dietary Fiber 0g); Protein 1g. **% Daily Value:** Vitamin A 0%; Vitamin C 0%; Calcium 2%; Iron 0%. **Diet Exchanges:** 1 Fat

*The start of a beautiful friendship—a 1933
box of Bisquick and busy bakers. Who could
be depressed when fresh biscuits from the
oven were just minutes away?*

Zucchini Bites

Beer-Battered Onion Rings with Cajun Dipping Sauce

5 servings

Vegetable oil

Cajun Dipping Sauce (below)

1 medium sweet onion (Vidalia or Texas), sliced and separated into rings

2 1/4 cups Original Bisquick

1 cup beer or nonalcoholic beer

1 teaspoon salt

2 eggs

1. Heat oil (1 1/2 inches) in deep fryer or heavy 3-quart saucepan to 375°. Make Cajun Dipping Sauce. Toss onion rings and 1/4 cup of the Bisquick.

2. Stir remaining 2 cups Bisquick, the beer, salt and eggs until smooth. (If batter is too thick, stir in additional beer, 1 tablespoon at a time, until desired consistency.) Dip onion rings, a few at a time, into batter, letting excess drip into bowl.

3. Fry about 2 minutes, turning with fork after 1 minute, until golden brown; drain on paper towels. Serve hot with dipping sauce.

Cajun Dipping Sauce

1/2 cup mayonnaise or salad dressing

1/2 cup sour cream

1/4 cup chili sauce

1 teaspoon prepared horseradish

1/4 teaspoon ground red pepper (cayenne)

Stir all ingredients until blended.

High Altitude (3500 to 6500 feet): No changes.
1 Serving: Calories 465 (Calories from Fat 305); Fat 34g (Saturated 8g); Cholesterol 90mg; Sodium 1270mg; Carbohydrate 35g (Dietary Fiber 1g); Protein 6g. **% Daily Value:** Vitamin A 8%; Vitamin C 2%; Calcium 12%; Iron 10%. **Diet Exchanges:** 1 Starch, 1 Vegetable, 7 Fat

Betty's Tip Nobody likes soggy onion rings. To keep your rings crispy and crunchy, make sure the oil is up to temperature (375°) before you begin frying. If you fry a large batch of rings, you may have to wait a few minutes for the oil to heat up before you begin again. The only way to really tell if the temperature is right is to use a special deep-fat or candy thermometer.

Beer-Battered Onion Rings with Cajun Dipping Sauce

All-Time
FAVORITE

Biscuits

9 biscuits

2 1/4 cups Original Bisquick

2/3 cup milk

1. Heat oven to 450°. Stir ingredients until soft dough forms.

2. Place dough on surface sprinkled with Bisquick; roll in Bisquick to coat. Shape into a ball; knead 10 times. Roll dough 1/2 inch thick. Cut with 2 1/2-inch round cutter dipped in Bisquick. Place on ungreased cookie sheet.

3. Bake 8 to 10 minutes or until golden brown.

High Altitude (3500 to 6500 feet): Heat oven to 475°.
1 Biscuit: Calories 135 (Calories from Fat 45); Fat 5g (Saturated 1g); Cholesterol 0mg; Sodium 430mg; Carbohydrate 19g (Dietary Fiber 0g); Protein 3g. **% Daily Value:** Vitamin A 0%; Vitamin C 0%; Calcium 6%; Iron 4%. **Diet Exchanges:** 1 Starch, 1 Fat

Drop Biscuits: Do not knead dough. Drop dough by 9 spoonfuls onto ungreased cookie sheet.

It takes just minutes to stir up a batch of homemade biscuits, with these easy biscuit basics:

1. Stir it up. Stir the ingredients with a spoon until a soft, slightly sticky dough forms. If the dough is too soft to handle, stir in 2 to 4 tablespoons of additional Bisquick.

2. Knead it. Sprinkle a surface with Bisquick and roll the dough in Bisquick to keep it from sticking. Dipping your fingers into a little Bisquick will also keep the dough from sticking to your hands. Then shape the dough into a ball, and knead it gently about ten times. Kneading helps develop the structure of the biscuit so they don't crumble and fall apart.

3. Roll the dough. For nice-looking biscuits and even baking, roll the dough about 1/2 inch thick. Here's a clever trick for rolling dough to the right thickness every time: Use two sticks, 1/2 inch thick and about 14 inches long, as a guide. Place the ball of dough between the sticks, and roll the dough to the thickness of the sticks.

4. Cut it out. Cut the dough with a round biscuit cutter dipped in Bisquick, pushing the cutter straight down through the dough. If you twist as you cut, the biscuits may be uneven. Cut the biscuits out of the dough as close together as possible. After cutting as many biscuits as possible, lightly press—don't knead—the scraps of dough together. Roll or pat the remaining dough until it is 1/2 inch thick, then cut. These biscuits may look slightly uneven.

5. The sheet is important. Place the biscuits about 1 inch apart on an ungreased cookie sheet. Shiny aluminum cookie sheets of good quality produce the best biscuits. If the cookie sheet is brown, black or darkened from a buildup of fat, the bottoms of the biscuits will be darker in color. Reducing the oven temperature to 400° may help. Also, be sure to place the cookie sheet on the center oven rack. That way, the biscuits will brown evenly on both the top and bottom.

✳ *Why are my biscuits heavy and why didn't they rise?*

• Not enough Bisquick or too much liquid.
• Too little or too gentle kneading.
• Dough stood too long before baking.

✳ *Why are my biscuits tough and hard?*

• Too much Bisquick or not enough liquid.
• Dough overmixed or kneaded too much.
• Oven too hot.
• Baked too long.

Savory Pull-Apart Bread

6 servings

10 sun-dried tomato halves
   (not packed in oil)

2 cups Original Bisquick

1 package (8 ounces) feta cheese,
   coarsely crumbled

3/4 cup milk

3/4 cup roasted red bell (sweet)
   peppers (from 7-ounce jar),
   drained and finely chopped

1 tablespoon chopped fresh or
   1 teaspoon dried oregano leaves

1 tablespoon chopped fresh or
   1 teaspoon dried basil leaves

1 clove garlic, finely chopped

2 tablespoons olive or vegetable oil

1. Heat oven to 425°. Grease square pan, 9 x 9 x 2 inches. Cover dried tomatoes with boiling water. Let stand 10 minutes; drain. Finely chop tomatoes.

2. Mix Bisquick, tomatoes, half of the cheese and the milk in medium bowl until dough forms. Mix remaining cheese, the bell peppers oregano, basil, garlic and oil in small bowl. Drop half of the dough by tablespoonfuls closely together in irregular pattern in pan. Spoon half of the cheese mixture over dough. Drop remaining dough over cheese mixture. Top with remaining cheese mixture.

3. Bake about 20 minutes or until golden brown. Serve warm.

High Altitude (3500 to 6500 feet): Use 2 1/4 cups Bisquick. Bake about 25 minutes. **1 Serving:** Calories 325 (Calories from Fat 170); Fat 19g (Saturated 8g); Cholesterol 35mg; Sodium 1060mg; Carbohydrate 30g (Dietary Fiber 1g); Protein 10g. **% Daily Value:** Vitamin A 12%; Vitamin C 24%; Calcium 0%; Iron 10%. **Diet Exchanges:** 1 1/2 Starch, 1 Vegetable, 4 Fat

Betty's Tip Using kitchen scissors makes the task of chopping dried tomatoes much easier. Try cutting them before soaking in boiling water.

Savory Pull-Apart Bread

Triple Cheese Flatbread

16 servings

2 cups Original Bisquick

1/2 cup hot water

2 tablespoons margarine or butter, melted

1/4 cup shredded Cheddar cheese (1 ounce)

1/4 cup shredded Monterey Jack cheese (1 ounce)

1/4 cup grated Parmesan cheese

1/2 teaspoon garlic powder

1/2 teaspoon Italian seasoning, if desired

1. Heat oven to 450°. Mix Bisquick and hot water until stiff dough forms. Let stand 10 minutes. Place dough on surface sprinkled with Bisquick; gently roll in Bisquick to coat. Shape into a ball; knead 60 times.

2. Roll or pat dough into 12-inch square on ungreased cookie sheet. Spread margarine over dough. Mix remaining ingredients; sprinkle over dough.

3. Bake 10 to 12 minutes or until edges are golden brown. Serve warm.

High Altitude (3500 to 6500 feet): No changes.
1 Serving: Calories 90 (Calories from Fat 45); Fat 5g (Saturated 2g); Cholesterol 5mg; Sodium 280mg; Carbohydrate 9g (Dietary Fiber 0g); Protein 2g. **% Daily Value:** Vitamin A 2%; Vitamin C 0%; Calcium 6%; Iron 2%. **Diet Exchanges:** 1/2 Starch, 1 Fat

Dreamboats from 1938 beg for biscuits—the way to a man's heart?

Triple Cheese Flatbread

Pepperoni-Cheese Breadsticks

About 20 breadsticks

2 3/4 cups Original Bisquick

1 cup shredded Monterey Jack
cheese (4 ounces)

1 medium onion, finely chopped

1/2 cup sour cream

1/2 cup buttermilk

1 clove garlic, finely chopped

1 package (3 ounces) sliced
pepperoni, chopped

1 cup grated Parmesan cheese

1. Heat oven to 375°. Grease 2 cookie sheets. Stir all ingredients except Parmesan cheese until dough forms.

2. Drop dough by heaping tablespoonfuls into Parmesan cheese. Roll in cheese to coat. Roll into 8-inch breadsticks. Place about 1 1/2 inches apart on cookie sheets.

3. Bake 15 to 18 minutes or until golden brown.

High Altitude (3500 to 6500 feet): No changes.
1 Breadstick: Calories 150 (Calories from Fat 80); Fat 9g (Saturated 4g); Cholesterol 15mg; Sodium 450mg; Carbohydrate 11g (Dietary Fiber 0g); Protein 6g. **% Daily Value:** Vitamin A 2%; Vitamin C 0%; Calcium 14%; Iron 4%. **Diet Exchanges:** 1 Starch, 1 1/2 Fat

Betty's Tip Do a little dipping! Spaghetti sauce, pizza sauce and cheese sauce are all wonderful dips, especially when served warm.

Pepperoni-Cheese Breadsticks

Corn Bread Sticks

16 corn bread sticks

1 cup Original Bisquick

1 cup yellow cornmeal

1 1/2 cups buttermilk

2 tablespoons vegetable oil

2 eggs

About 2 tablespoons yellow cornmeal

1. Heat oven to 450°. Grease 2 loaf pans, 9 x 5 x 3 inches.

2. Stir Bisquick, 1 cup cornmeal, the buttermilk, oil and eggs until blended. Pour into pans. Sprinkle with 2 tablespoons cornmeal.

3. Bake about 15 minutes or until toothpick inserted in center comes out clean. Remove from pans. Cut each loaf crosswise into 8 sticks.

High Altitude (3500 to 6500 feet): Bake about 20 minutes.
1 Stick: Calories 95 (Calories from Fat 35); Fat 4g (Saturated 1g); Cholesterol 30mg; Sodium 130mg; Carbohydrate 13g (Dietary Fiber 1g); Protein 3g. **% Daily Value:** Vitamin A 2%; Vitamin C 0%; Calcium 4%; Iron 4%. **Diet Exchanges:** 1 Starch, 1/2 Fat

Betty's Tip These hearty corn sticks are simply superb spread with honey-butter or drizzled with maple syrup. They also make dynamite dunkers dipped into a bowl of steaming chili.

Corn Bread Sticks

family-pleasing
dinners

Stuffed-Crust Pizza (page 106), Family Favorite Stew (page 107)

Stuffed-Crust Pizza

8 servings

3 cups Original Bisquick

2/3 cup very hot water

2 tablespoons vegetable oil

4 smoked string cheese pieces, cut lengthwise in half (from 8-ounce package)

1 can (8 ounces) pizza sauce

1/2 package (3-ounce size) sliced Canadian-style bacon

1/2 cup sliced mushrooms

1/3 cup chopped bell pepper

1/4 cup sliced ripe olives

1 1/2 cups shredded mozzarella cheese (6 ounces)

1. Stir Bisquick, hot water and oil until soft dough forms; beat vigorously 20 strokes. Let stand 8 minutes.

2. Heat oven to 450°. Grease 12-inch pizza pan. Press dough in bottom and 1 inch over side of pizza pan, using fingers dusted with Bisquick. Place string cheese along edge of dough. Fold 1 inch edge of dough over and around cheese; press to seal. Bake 7 minutes.

3. Spread pizza sauce over crust. Top with bacon, mushrooms, bell pepper and olives. Sprinkle with mozzarella cheese. Bake 8 to 10 minutes or until crust is golden brown and cheese is melted.

High Altitude (3500 to 6500 feet): No changes.
1 Serving: Calories 310 (Calories from Fat 145); Fat 16g (Saturated 5g); Cholesterol 20mg; Sodium 950mg; Carbohydrate 31g (Dietary Fiber 1g); Protein 12g. **% Daily Value:** Vitamin A 6%; Vitamin C 6%; Calcium 28%; Iron 10%. **Diet Exchanges:** 2 Starch, 1 High-Fat Meat, 1 Fat.

Betty's Tip Like your pizza extra crispy? For a crisper crust, sprinkle half of the mozzarella cheese on the partially baked crust. Top with pizza sauce, bacon and mushrooms, and sprinkle with the remaining cheese.

Family-Favorite Stew

6 servings

1 pound ground beef

2 cups water

2 cans (14 1/2 ounces each) diced
   tomatoes in olive oil, garlic and
   spices, undrained

1 can (6 ounces) tomato paste

1 bag (16 ounces) frozen carrots,
   green beans and cauliflower
   (or other combination)

2 1/4 cups Original Bisquick

2/3 cup milk

1 tablespoon chopped fresh parsley

1. Heat oven to 425°. Cook beef in ovenproof 4-quart Dutch oven over medium heat, stirring occasionally, until brown; drain. Stir in water, tomatoes, tomato paste and vegetables. Heat to boiling, stirring occasionally.

2. Mix Bisquick, milk and parsley until soft dough forms. Drop dough by 6 spoonfuls onto beef mixture; remove from heat.

3. Bake uncovered 20 to 25 minutes or until biscuits are golden brown and stew is bubbly.

High Altitude (3500 to 6500 feet): Heat oven to 450°.
1 Serving: Calories 430 (Calories from Fat 170); Fat 19g (Saturated 6g); Cholesterol 45mg; Sodium 1310mg; Carbohydrate 48g (Dietary Fiber 5g); Protein 22g. **% Daily Value:** Vitamin A 38%; Vitamin C 44%; Calcium 18%; Iron 22%. **Diet Exchanges:** 2 Starch, 1 1/2 High-Fat Meat, 3 Vegetable, 1 Fat.

Betty's Tip Go ahead and substitute ground turkey for the ground beef in this recipe for a tasty new twist.

Chili with Corn Dumplings

6 servings

1 1/2 pounds ground beef

1 large onion, chopped (3/4 cup)

1 can (15 1/4 ounces) whole kernel corn, undrained

1 can (14 1/2 ounces) stewed tomatoes, undrained

1 can (16 ounces) tomato sauce

2 tablespoons chili powder

1 teaspoon red pepper sauce

1 1/3 cups Original Bisquick

2/3 cup cornmeal

2/3 cup milk

3 tablespoons chopped fresh cilantro or parsley, if desired

1. Cook beef and onion in 4-quart Dutch oven over medium heat, stirring occasionally, until beef is brown; drain. Reserve 1/2 cup of the corn. Stir remaining corn with liquid, tomatoes, tomato sauce, chili powder and pepper sauce into beef mixture. Heat to boiling; reduce heat. Cover and simmer 15 minutes.

2. Mix Bisquick and cornmeal. Stir in milk, cilantro and reserved 1/2 cup corn just until moistened.

3. Heat chili to boiling. Drop dough by rounded tablespoonfuls onto chili; reduce heat to low. Cook uncovered 10 minutes. Cover and cook about 10 minutes longer or until dumplings are dry.

High Altitude (3500 to 6500 feet): After dropping dough onto chili, cook uncovered over low heat 15 minutes. Cover and cook 15 to 18 minutes longer or until dumplings are dry.

1 Serving: Calories 515 (Calories from Fat 200); Fat 22g (Saturated 8g); Cholesterol 65mg; Sodium 1310mg; Carbohydrate 56g (Dietary Fiber 6g); Protein 29g. **% Daily Value:** Vitamin A 22%; Vitamin C 24%; Calcium 12%; Iron 28%. **Diet Exchanges:** 3 Starch, 2 High-Fat Meat, 2 Vegetable, 1 Fat.

Betty's Tip Feel free to use either white or yellow cornmeal to make this mildly spicy main dish. You can also use 2 cups of frozen corn instead of the canned corn.

Chili with Corn Dumplings

Sloppy Joe Bake
6 servings

1 pound ground beef

1 can (15 1/2 ounces) original-style sloppy joe sauce

2 cups Original Bisquick

1/2 cup milk

2 tablespoons margarine or butter, softened

1 egg

4 slices process American cheese, cut diagonally in half

1. Heat oven to 375°. Grease round pan, 9 x 1 1/2 inches. Make beef and sloppy joe sauce as directed on can.

2. Stir Bisquick, milk, margarine and egg until soft dough forms. Spread dough in bottom and up side of pan to within 1/4 inch of rim. Spoon beef mixture evenly over dough.

3. Bake uncovered 25 minutes. Arrange cheese triangles on beef mixture. Bake about 5 minutes or until cheese is melted.

High Altitude (3500 to 6500 feet): Heat oven to 400°.
1 Serving: Calories 310 (Calories from Fat 135); Fat 15g (Saturated 5g); Cholesterol 80mg; Sodium 700mg; Carbohydrate 27g (Dietary Fiber 1g); Protein 18g. **% Daily Value:** Vitamin A 6%; Vitamin C 6%; Calcium 8%; Iron 14%. **Diet Exchanges:** 2 Starch, 2 Medium-Fat Meat.

In the 1990s, soccer moms—and dads— score a goal every time with Bisquick.

Sloppy Joe Bake

Quick Cheeseburger Bake

8 servings

1 pound ground beef

1 large onion, chopped (3/4 cup)

1 can (11 ounces) condensed
   Cheddar cheese soup

1 cup frozen peas and carrots,
   if desired

1/4 cup milk

2 cups Original Bisquick

3/4 cup water

1 cup shredded Cheddar cheese
   (4 ounces)

1. Heat oven to 400°. Grease rectangular baking dish, 13 x 9 x 2 inches. Cook beef and onion in 10-inch skillet over medium heat, stirring occasionally, until beef is brown; drain. Stir in soup, vegetables and milk; remove from heat.

2. Stir Bisquick and water in baking dish until moistened; spread evenly. Spread beef mixture over batter. Sprinkle with cheese.

3. Bake uncovered 30 minutes.

High Altitude (3500 to 6500 feet): No changes.
1 Serving: Calories 340 (Calories from Fat 180); Fat 20g (Saturated 9g); Cholesterol 55mg; Sodium 890mg; Carbohydrate 23g (Dietary Fiber 1g); Protein 18g. **% Daily Value:** Vitamin A 12%; Vitamin C 0%; Calcium 16%; Iron 12%. **Diet Exchanges:** 1 1/2 Starch, 2 High-Fat Meat, 1/2 Fat.

Betty's Tip If you aren't fond of onions, you can leave them out or substitute 3/4 cup sliced fresh mushrooms.

Quick Cheeseburger Bake

Beef Stroganoff Casserole

4 servings

1 pound beef sirloin steak, about 1/2 inch thick

2 tablespoons margarine or butter

1 package (8 ounces) sliced mush-rooms (3 cups)

1 medium onion, chopped (1/2 cup)

3/4 cup beef broth

1/2 teaspoon Worcestershire sauce

1/4 teaspoon salt

1 cup sour cream

1 cup Original Bisquick

1/4 cup milk

1 egg

1. Heat oven to 400°. Grease 2 1/2-quart casserole. Cut beef into 1 x 1/2-inch pieces. Melt margarine in 10-inch skillet over medium-high heat. Cook mushrooms and onion in margarine, stirring constantly, until onion is tender; remove from skillet.

2. Cook beef in same skillet, stirring occasionally, until brown. Stir in broth, Worcestershire sauce and salt. Heat to boiling; reduce heat. Cover and simmer 15 minutes. Stir in mushroom mixture. Heat to boiling, stirring constantly; remove from heat. Stir in sour cream. Spoon mixture into casserole.

3. Stir remaining ingredients until blended. Spread evenly over beef mixture. Bake uncovered 20 to 25 minutes or until topping is golden brown. Let stand 5 minutes before serving.

High Altitude (3500 to 6500 feet): No changes.
1 Serving: Calories 450 (Calories from Fat 235); Fat 26g (Saturated 11g); Cholesterol 145mg; Sodium 940mg; Carbohydrate 27g (Dietary Fiber 1g); Protein 28g. **% Daily Value:** Vitamin A 18%; Vitamin C 2%; Calcium 14%; Iron 20%. **Diet Exchanges:** 1 1/2 Starch, 3 Medium-Fat Meat, 1 Vegetable, 2 Fat.

Betty's Tip Wild about mushrooms? Try sliced shiitake or portabella mushrooms for a rich and hearty flavor.

Beef Stroganoff Casserole

Steak Bake

6 servings

1 pound beef sirloin steak, about 1/2 inch thick

1/4 cup Original Bisquick

1/4 teaspoon pepper

2 tablespoons vegetable oil

1 bag (16 ounces) frozen green beans, potatoes, onions and red peppers (or other combination), thawed

1 can (14 1/2 ounces) diced tomatoes, undrained

1/4 cup water

1 1/2 tablespoons soy sauce

1 1/2 tablespoons molasses

1 cup Original Bisquick

1/3 cup milk

1/4 teaspoon ground mustard

1 egg

1 tablespoon sesame seed, if desired

1. Heat oven to 400°. Cut beef into 1-inch pieces. Mix beef, 1/4 cup Bisquick and the pepper until beef is coated. Heat oil in 10-inch nonstick skillet over medium heat. Cook beef in oil, stirring occasionally, until brown.

2. Mix beef, vegetables, tomatoes, water, soy sauce and molasses in ungreased rectangular baking dish, 13 x 9 x 2 inches. Bake uncovered 15 minutes; stir.

3. Stir 1 cup Bisquick, the milk, mustard and egg until blended. Drop dough by 6 spoonfuls onto beef mixture. Sprinkle sesame seed over dough. Bake uncovered 20 to 25 minutes or until biscuits are golden brown.

High Altitude (3500 to 6500 feet): No changes.
1 Serving: Calories 265 (Calories from Fat 80); Fat 9g (Saturated 2g); Cholesterol 70mg; Sodium 730mg; Carbohydrate 30g (Dietary Fiber 2g); Protein 18g. **% Daily Value:** Vitamin A 12%; Vitamin C 36%; Calcium 10%; Iron 16%. **Diet Exchanges:** 1 Starch, 1 Lean Meat, 3 Vegetable, 1 Fat.

Betty's Tip You'll find beef is easier to cut if it's partially frozen. Just pop it in the freezer about 1 1/2 hours before you plan to slice it up for this recipe.

Steak Bake

Roast Beef and Swiss Sandwich Bake

6 servings

2 cups Original Bisquick

1 cup milk

2 tablespoons yellow mustard

1 egg

1 package (6 ounces) thinly sliced
cooked roast beef, chopped

1 cup shredded Swiss cheese
(4 ounces)

Freshly ground pepper, if desired

1. Heat oven to 350°. Grease square baking dish, 8 x 8 x 2 inches.

2. Stir Bisquick, milk, mustard and egg until blended. Pour half of the batter into baking dish. Top with half of the roast beef and 1/2 cup of the cheese. Top with remaining roast beef. Pour remaining batter over roast beef.

3. Bake uncovered 45 to 50 minutes or until golden brown and center is set. Sprinkle with remaining 1/2 cup cheese and the pepper. Let stand 5 minutes before serving.

High Altitude (3500 to 6500 feet): Sprinkle with cheese to within 1/4 inch of edges of baking dish. Bake 47 to 52 minutes.

1 Serving: Calories 330 (Calories from Fat 155); Fat 17g (Saturated 7g); 75mg; Sodium 730mg; Carbohydrate 27g (Dietary Fiber 1g); Protein 18g. **% Daily Value:** Vitamin A 6%; Vitamin C 4%; Calcium 22%; Iron 10%. **Diet Exchanges:** 1 Starch, 1 1/2 High-Fat Meat, 2 Vegetable, 1 Fat.

Betty's Tip Vary this dish by using thinly sliced cooked turkey or chicken instead of roast beef and shredded Cheddar cheese instead of Swiss.

Roast Beef and Swiss Sandwich Bake

Breaded Pork Chops

8 servings

1/2 cup Original Bisquick

12 saltine crackers, crushed
(1/2 cup)

1 teaspoon seasoned salt

1/4 teaspoon pepper

1 egg

2 tablespoons water

8 pork boneless loin chops,
1/2 inch thick (about 2 pounds)

1. Mix Bisquick, cracker crumbs, seasoned salt and pepper. Mix egg and water.

2. Dip pork into egg mixture, then coat with Bisquick mixture.

3. Spray 12-inch nonstick skillet with cooking spray; heat over medium-high heat. Cook pork in skillet 8 to 10 minutes, turning once, until slightly pink in center.

High Altitude (3500 to 6500 feet): No changes.
1 Serving: Calories 215 (Calories from Fat 90); Fat 10g (Saturated 3g); Cholesterol 90mg; Sodium 370mg; Carbohydrate 7g (Dietary Fiber 0g); Protein 24g. **% Daily Value:** Vitamin A 0%; Vitamin C 0%; Calcium 2%; Iron 6%. **Diet Exchanges:** 1/2 Starch, 3 Lean Meat.

A hint to all wives in the 1940s —be kind to your husband with great Bisquick meals, and he'll be sure to return the favor.

Breaded Pork Chops

Italian Sausage Pot Pies

4 servings

1 pound bulk Italian sausage or ground beef

1 medium onion, chopped (1/2 cup)

1 small green bell pepper, chopped (1/2 cup)

1/2 cup sliced mushrooms

1 can (8 ounces) pizza sauce

1 cup shredded mozzarella cheese (4 ounces)

1 cup Original Bisquick

1/4 cup boiling water

1. Heat oven to 375°. Grease four 10- to 12-ounce casseroles. Cook sausage, onion and bell pepper in 10-inch skillet over medium heat, stirring frequently, until sausage is no longer pink; drain. Stir in mushrooms and pizza sauce. Heat to boiling; reduce heat. Simmer uncovered 5 minutes, stirring occasionally. Spoon sausage mixture into casseroles. Sprinkle 1/4 cup of the cheese over each.

2. Stir Bisquick and boiling water; beat vigorously 20 strokes. Place dough on surface sprinkled with Bisquick; gently roll in Bisquick to coat. Shape into a ball; knead about 10 times or until smooth.

3. Divide dough into 4 balls. Pat each ball into circle the size of the diameter of the casseroles. Make cut in each circle with knife to vent steam. Place circles on sausage mixture in casseroles. Bake 15 to 20 minutes or until light golden brown.

High Altitude (3500 to 6500 feet): Bake 22 to 25 minutes.
1 Serving: Calories 520 (Calories from Fat 295); Fat 33g (Saturated 12g); Cholesterol 80mg; Sodium 1540mg; Carbohydrate 29g (Dietary Fiber 2g); Protein 28g. **% Daily Value:** Vitamin A 8%; Vitamin C 28%; Calcium 28%; Iron 16%. **Diet Exchanges:** 2 Starch, 3 High-Fat Meat, 1 1/2 Fat.

Betty's Tip For a special holiday treat, use a small cookie cutter to cut a festive shape out of the dough circle before putting it on the sausage mixture. For itty-bitty pastry treats, place the cut-outs on a cookie sheet and bake in a 375° oven about 15 minutes or until light golden brown.

Italian Sausage Pot Pies

Oven-Fried Chicken

6 servings

1 tablespoon margarine or butter

2/3 cup Original Bisquick

1 1/2 teaspoons paprika

1 1/4 teaspoons salt

1/4 teaspoon pepper

3- to 3 1/2-pound cut-up broiler-fryer chicken

1. Heat oven to 425°. Melt margarine in rectangular baking dish or pan, 13 x 9 x 2 inches, in oven.

2. Mix Bisquick, paprika, salt and pepper. Coat chicken with Bisquick. Place skin sides down in pan (pan and margarine should be hot).

3. Bake uncovered 35 minutes; turn chicken. Bake about 15 minutes longer or until juice of chicken is no longer pink when centers of thickest pieces are cut.

High Altitude (3500 to 6500 feet): Bake 40 minutes; turn chicken. Bake about 20 minutes longer.
1 Serving: Calories 295 (Calories from Fat 155); Fat 17g (Saturated 4g); Cholesterol 85mg; Sodium 785mg; Carbohydrate 8g (Dietary Fiber 0g); Protein 28g. **% Daily Value:** Vitamin A 10%; Vitamin C %; Calcium 4%; Iron 10%. **Diet Exchanges:** 1/2 Starch, 4 Lean Meat, 1 Fat.

Mexican Oven-Fried Chicken: Decrease Bisquick to 1/2 cup. Add 2 tablespoons yellow cornmeal and 1 to 2 tablespoons chili powder.

Parmesan Oven-Fried Chicken: Decrease Bisquick to 1/3 cup and salt to 1 teaspoon. Add 1/2 cup grated Parmesan cheese.

Betty's Tip For a dynamite, down-home meal, serve this crispy chicken with biscuits, steamed veggies and a spoonful of barbecue sauce on the side.

Oven-Fried Chicken

Cajun Chicken

4 servings

4 boneless, skinless chicken breast halves (about 1 1/4 pounds)

1 1/2 cups cornflakes cereal, crushed (1/2 cup)

1/2 cup Original Bisquick

2 teaspoons Cajun seasoning

1/2 cup water

2 tablespoons margarine or butter

1. Flatten each chicken breast half to about 1/4-inch thickness between sheets of waxed paper or plastic wrap.

2. Mix cereal, Bisquick and Cajun seasoning. Dip chicken into water, then coat with cereal mixture.

3. Melt margarine in 12-inch nonstick skillet over medium heat. Cook chicken in margarine 8 to 10 minutes, turning once, until juice is no longer pink when centers of thickest pieces are cut.

High Altitude (3500 to 6500 feet): Cook chicken 10 to 12 minutes.
1 Serving: Calories 275 (Calories from Fat 90); Fat 10g (Saturated 2g); Cholesterol 75mg; Sodium 450mg; Carbohydrate 18g (Dietary Fiber 1g); Protein 28g. **% Daily Value:** Vitamin A 18%; Vitamin C 2%; Calcium 4%; Iron 26%. **Diet Exchanges:** 1 Starch, 4 Lean Meat.

Betty's Tip For a southern-style chicken sandwich, serve in toasted sesame buns with barbecue sauce, lettuce, red onion and tomato slices.

Cajun Chicken

Thai Chicken with Spicy Peanut Sauce

4 servings

3 tablespoons margarine or butter

1 cup Original Bisquick

1 1/2 teaspoons curry powder

1 1/2 teaspoons garlic powder

1 teaspoon ground ginger

4 boneless, skinless chicken breast halves (about 1 1/4 pounds)

1/3 cup milk

Spicy Peanut Sauce (below)

2 tablespoons cocktail peanuts, finely chopped

1. Heat oven to 425°. Melt margarine in rectangular baking dish, 13 x 9 x 2 inches, in oven.

2. Mix Bisquick, curry powder, garlic powder and ginger. Dip chicken into milk, then coat with Bisquick mixture. Place in dish.

3. Bake uncovered 20 minutes; turn chicken. Bake about 10 minutes longer or until juice of chicken is no longer pink when centers of thickest pieces are cut. While chicken is baking, make Spicy Peanut Sauce. Serve sauce over chicken. Sprinkle with peanuts.

Spicy Peanut Sauce

1/2 cup plain yogurt

1/4 cup creamy peanut butter

1/2 cup milk

1 tablespoon soy sauce

1/8 teaspoon ground red pepper (cayenne)

Mix all ingredients in 10-inch nonstick skillet. Cook over medium heat 3 to 4 minutes, stirring occasionally, until mixture begins to thicken.

High Altitude (3500 to 6500 feet): No changes.
1 Serving: Calories 510 (Calories from Fat 260); Fat 29g (Saturated 7g); Cholesterol 0mg; Sodium 950mg; Carbohydrate 27g (Dietary Fiber 2g); Protein 37g. **% Daily Value:** Vitamin A 16%; Vitamin C 0%; Calcium 18%; Iron 14%. **Diet Exchanges:** 1 1/2 Starch, 5 Lean Meat, 3 Fat.

Betty's Tip Entertaining? Serve this spicy chicken over hot cooked jasmine rice with steamed carrots and broccoli or broccolini, a new kind of broccoli, with sparse flowerets.

Thai Chicken with Spicy Peanut Sauce

Lemon-Apricot Chicken

4 servings

4 boneless, skinless chicken breast halves (about 1 1/4 pounds)

1/4 cup margarine or butter, melted

1 egg

2 tablespoons water

1 cup Original Bisquick

1 tablespoon grated lemon peel

1/4 teaspoon garlic powder

Lemon-Apricot Sauce (below)

1. Heat oven to 425°. Flatten each chicken breast half to 1/2-inch thickness between sheets of plastic wrap or waxed paper. Spread 1 tablespoon of the melted margarine in jelly roll pan, 15 1/2 x 10 1/2 x 1 inch.

2. Beat egg and water slightly. Mix Bisquick, lemon peel and garlic powder. Dip chicken into egg mixture, then coat with Bisquick mixture. Place in pan. Drizzle with remaining melted margarine.

3. Bake uncovered 20 minutes; turn chicken. Bake about 10 minutes longer or until juice of chicken is no longer pink when centers of thickest pieces are cut. Make Lemon-Apricot Sauce. Cut chicken crosswise into 1/2-inch slices. Pour sauce over chicken.

Lemon-Apricot Sauce

2/3 cup apricot preserves

2 tablespoons lemon juice

1/2 teaspoon soy sauce

1/4 teaspoon ground ginger

Heat all ingredients in 1-quart saucepan over medium heat, stirring occasionally, until warm.

High Altitude (3500 to 6500 feet): No changes.
1 Serving: Calories 340 (Calories from Fat 125); Fat 14g (Saturated 4g); Cholesterol 80mg; Sodium 470mg; Carbohydrate 36g (Dietary Fiber 1g); Protein 19g. **% Daily Value:** Vitamin A 12%; Vitamin C 4%; Calcium 6%; Iron 8%. **Diet Exchanges:** 2 Starch, 2 Lean Meat, 1/2 Fruit, 1 Fat.

Betty's Tip Serve this citrus-kissed chicken with a side of hot cooked rice. Want to try something a little different? Fried rice makes a nice accompaniment.

Lemon-Apricot Chicken

All-Time
FAVORITE

Chicken and Dumplings

4 servings

1 1/2 cups milk

1 cup frozen peas and carrots

1 cup cut-up cooked chicken

1 can (10 3/4 ounces) condensed
   cream of chicken and
   mushroom soup

1 cup Original Bisquick

1/3 cup milk

Paprika, if desired

1. Heat 1 1/2 cups milk, the peas and carrots, chicken and soup to boiling in 3-quart saucepan.

2. Stir Bisquick and 1/3 cup milk until soft dough forms. Drop dough by 8 spoonfuls onto chicken mixture; reduce heat to low.

3. Cook uncovered 10 minutes. Cover and cook 10 minutes longer. Sprinkle with paprika.

High Altitude (3500 to 6500 feet): No changes.
1 Serving: Calories 315 (Calories from Fat 115); Fat 13g (Saturated 4g); Cholesterol 40mg; Sodium 1070mg; Carbohydrate 33g (Dietary Fiber 2g); Protein 18g. **% Daily Value:** Vitamin A 52%; Vitamin C 2%; Calcium 24%; Iron 12%. **Diet Exchanges:** 2 Starch, 2 Medium-Fat Meat.

Light and tender dumplings are a welcome addition to many soups, stews and chilies. Plus they're as easy to make as 1-2-3:

1. Stir it up. Stir the ingredients with a spoon just until a soft dough forms. Be careful not to mix the dough too much or the dumplings will turn out tough and heavy.

2. Hot, hot, hot! Be sure the liquid is hot before you add the dumpling dough. You can tell if the temperature is hot enough when the liquid is gently boiling with bubbles breaking on the surface. If you add the dough before the liquid is hot enough, the dumplings will be end up soggy and undercooked.

3. Drop 'em on top. Drop the dough by spoonfuls onto the meat or vegetables in the stew, not into the gravy or liquid. If the dough is dropped right into the liquid, the simmering action may break up the dumplings. Also, the dough will soak up moisture from the liquid so the dumplings will become soft and soggy.

✳ *Why are my dumplings tough, heavy and raw in the center?*

• Too much Bisquick or not enough liquid.
• Dough overmixed.
• Dumplings too large.
• Dough added to stew too soon.
• Dumplings not cooked properly (stew should continue to boil gently).

✳ *Why are my dumplings soggy and why did they fall apart?*

• Not enough Bisquick or too much liquid
• Dough dropped directly onto the hot liquid.

Easy Chicken Pot Pie

6 servings

1 cup cut-up cooked chicken

1 bag (16 ounces) frozen peas and carrots, thawed

1 can (10 3/4 ounces) condensed cream of chicken soup

1 cup Original Bisquick

1/2 cup milk

1 egg

1. Heat oven to 400°. Stir chicken, vegetables and soup in ungreased 2-quart casserole.

2. Stir remaining ingredients until blended. Pour over chicken mixture.

3. Bake uncovered about 30 minutes or until crust is golden brown.

High Altitude (3500 to 6500 feet): Heat oven to 425°.
1 Serving: Calories 200 (Calories from Fat 80); Fat 9g (Saturated 3g); Cholesterol 60mg; Sodium 730mg; Carbohydrate 19g (Dietary Fiber 1g); Protein 11g. **% Daily Value:** Vitamin A 12%; Vitamin C 6%; Calcium 6%; Iron 8%. **Diet Exchanges:** 1 Starch, 1 Lean Meat, 1 Vegetable, 1 Fat.

In 1996, Bisquick makes light work of stuffy cooking, and ushers in great taste without all the work.

Easy Chicken Pot Pie

Tuscan Chicken Torta

6 servings

1 can (15 to 16 ounces) cannellini beans, rinsed and drained

1 1/3 cups Original Bisquick

1/3 cup Italian dressing

1 1/2 cups diced cooked chicken

1 package (10 ounces) frozen chopped spinach, thawed and squeezed to drain

1 cup shredded mozzarella cheese (4 ounces)

3 eggs

1 1/4 cups milk

1/3 cup slivered almonds, toasted (page 18)

1. Heat oven to 375°. Mash beans in medium bowl. Stir in Bisquick and dressing. Spread in bottom and 2 inches up side of ungreased springform pan, 9 x 3 inches. Bake 10 to 12 minutes or until set.

2. Layer chicken, spinach and cheese over crust. Mix eggs and milk; pour over cheese. Sprinkle almonds evenly over top.

3. Bake uncovered 50 to 55 minutes or until golden brown and knife inserted near center comes out clean. Let stand 10 minutes. Loosen edge of torta from side of pan; remove side of pan.

High Altitude (3500 to 6500 feet): Bake about 55 minutes in step 3.
1 Serving: Calories 465 (Calories from Fat 200); Fat 22g (Saturated 6g); Cholesterol 150mg; Sodium 700mg; Carbohydrate 42g (Dietary Fiber 6g); Protein 31g. **% Daily Value:** Vitamin A 32%; Vitamin C 2%; Calcium 38%; Iron 26%. **Diet Exchanges:** 2 Starch, 3 Lean Meat, 2 Vegetable, 2 Fat.

Betty's Tip Cannellini beans are large, white Italian kidney beans. They are particularly popular in soups and salads, but in this recipe, they are mashed to help form a delicious crust.

Tuscan Chicken Torta

California Pizza

8 servings

1 can (8 ounces) tomato sauce

1 teaspoon dried oregano leaves

1/2 teaspoon dried basil leaves

1/2 teaspoon salt

1/4 teaspoon garlic or onion powder

1/8 teaspoon pepper

2 cups Original Bisquick

1/2 cup cold water

1 1/2 cups shredded Monterey Jack cheese (6 ounces)

2 cups cut-up cooked chicken

1/2 cup sliced ripe olives

1 medium avocado, sliced

1. Heat oven to 425°. Grease 12-inch pizza pan. Mix tomato sauce, oregano, basil, salt, garlic powder and pepper; set aside.

2. Mix Bisquick and cold water until soft dough forms. Press dough in pizza pan, using fingers dusted with Bisquick; pinch edge to form 1/2-inch rim. Sprinkle 1/2 cup of the cheese over dough. Spread tomato sauce over cheese. Top with chicken and olives. Sprinkle with remaining 1 cup cheese.

3. Bake 20 to 25 minutes or until crust is golden brown and cheese is bubbly. Garnish with avocado slices.

High Altitude (3500 to 6500 feet): Use boiling water to make dough.
1 Serving: Calories 310 (Calories from Fat 155); Fat 17g (Saturated 6g); Cholesterol 50mg; Sodium 980mg; Carbohydrate 23g (Dietary Fiber 2g); Protein 18g. **% Daily Value:** Vitamin A 12%; Vitamin C 4%; Calcium 22%; Iron 12%. **Diet Exchanges:** 1 1/2 Starch, 2 Medium-Fat Meat, 1 Fat.

Betty's Tip Need some avocado advice? Choose avocados that are heavy for their size and don't have nicks or bruises. Store unripe avocados at room temperature and ripe ones in the refrigerator for up to a week. If you want to speed up the ripening process, place avocados in a paper bag and let them stand at room temperature for a couple of days.

California Pizza

Barbecued Turkey Bake

6 servings

1 1/2 cups cut-up cooked turkey

1/3 cup chili sauce

2 tablespoons honey

1 teaspoon soy sauce

1/4 teaspoon red pepper sauce

1 small onion, sliced and separated
   into rings

1 1/2 cups Original Bisquick

1/3 cup cold water

1 cup shredded mozzarella cheese
   (4 ounces)

1. Heat oven to 375°. Mix turkey, chili sauce, honey, soy sauce, pepper sauce and onion; set aside.

2. Mix Bisquick and cold water until dough forms; beat 20 strokes. Roll or pat dough into 12 x 6-inch rectangle on ungreased cookie sheet; pinch edge to form 1/2-inch rim. Spoon turkey mixture onto dough.

3. Bake 25 minutes or until edge of crust is light brown. Sprinkle with cheese. Bake about 5 minutes or until cheese is melted.

High Altitude (3500 to 6500 feet): Heat oven to 400°.
1 Serving: Calories 275 (Calories from Fat 90); Fat 10g (Saturated 4g); Cholesterol 40mg; Sodium 790mg; Carbohydrate 30g (Dietary Fiber 1g); Protein 17g. **% Daily Value:** Vitamin A 4%; Vitamin C 2%; Calcium 20%; Iron 8%. **Diet Exchanges:** 2 Starch, 1 1/2 Medium-Fat Meat.

Betty's Tip When it's refrigerated, honey crystallizes, forming a gooey, grainy mess. Instead, store honey in an airtight container in a dry place at room temperature for up to a year.

Barbecued Turkey Bake

Turkey Club Squares

6 servings

2 cups Original Bisquick

1/3 cup mayonnaise or salad dressing

1/3 cup milk

2 cups cubed cooked turkey

2 medium green onions, sliced (2 tablespoons)

6 slices bacon, crisply cooked and crumbled

1/4 cup mayonnaise or salad dressing

1 large tomato, chopped (1 cup)

1 cup shredded Colby-Monterey Jack cheese (4 ounces)

1. Heat oven to 450°. Grease cookie sheet. Mix Bisquick, 1/3 cup mayonnaise and the milk until soft dough forms. Roll or pat dough into 12 x 8-inch rectangle on cookie sheet. Bake 8 to 10 minutes or until golden brown.

2. Mix turkey, onions, bacon and 1/4 cup mayonnaise. Spoon over crust to within 1/4 inch of edges. Sprinkle with tomato and cheese.

3. Bake 5 to 6 minutes or until turkey mixture is hot and cheese is melted.

High Altitude (3500 to 6500 feet): Bake crust about 10 minutes in step 1. Bake 6 to 8 minutes in step 3.

1 Serving: Calories 525 (Calories from Fat 325); Fat 36g (Saturated 11g); Cholesterol 80mg; Sodium 960mg; Carbohydrate 28g (Dietary Fiber 1g); Protein 23g. **% Daily Value:** Vitamin A 8%; Vitamin C 4%; Calcium 20%; Iron 12%. **Diet Exchanges:** 2 Starch, 2 1/2 High-Fat Meat, 2 1/2 Fat.

Betty's Tip Purchase cooked turkey at the deli or prepackaged in the meat department to make this tasty brunch or supper dish in a snap.

Turkey Club Squares

Turkey and Corn Bread Stuffing Casserole

6 servings

1 can (10 3/4 ounces) condensed cream of chicken or celery soup

1 1/4 cups milk

1 cup frozen green peas

1/2 cup dried cranberries

4 medium green onions, sliced (1/4 cup)

2 cups cut-up cooked turkey or chicken

1 1/2 cups corn bread stuffing mix

1 cup Original Bisquick

1/4 cup milk

2 eggs

1. Heat oven to 400°. Grease 3-quart casserole. Heat soup and milk to boiling in 3-quart saucepan, stirring frequently. Stir in peas, cranberries and onions. Heat to boiling, stirring frequently; remove from heat. Stir in turkey and stuffing mix. Spoon into casserole.

2. Stir remaining ingredients until blended. Pour over stuffing mixture.

3. Bake uncovered 35 to 40 minutes or until knife inserted in center comes out clean.

High Altitude (3500 to 6500 feet): Use 1 1/2 cups milk instead of 1 1/4 cups.
1 Serving: Calories 505 (Calories from Fat 215); Fat 24g (Saturated 7g); Cholesterol 150mg; Sodium 1050mg; Carbohydrate 53g (Dietary Fiber 6g); Protein 25g. **% Daily Value:** Vitamin A 22%; Vitamin C 14%; Calcium 24%; Iron 18%. **Diet Exchanges:** 3 Starch, 2 Lean Meat, 1 Vegetable, 3 Fat.

Betty's Tip Make a mid-week meal special by serving this cozy casserole with a side of cranberry-orange relish or cranberry sauce.

Turkey and Corn Bread Stuffing Casserole

Hot Turkey Salad with Sage Biscuits

6 servings

1/4 cup mayonnaise or salad dressing

2 tablespoons Original Bisquick

2 cups cut-up cooked turkey

1/4 cup shredded Cheddar cheese (1 ounce)

2 medium stalks celery, sliced (1 cup)

2 medium green onions, sliced (2 tablespoons)

2 1/4 cups Original Bisquick

3/4 cup milk

1/2 teaspoon dried sage leaves

1. Heat oven to 425°. Mix mayonnaise and 2 tablespoons Bisquick in medium bowl until well blended. Stir in turkey, cheese, celery and onions; set aside.

2. Mix remaining ingredients just until soft dough forms. Place on surface sprinkled with Bisquick; roll in Bisquick to coat. Shape into a ball; knead 10 times. Roll dough 1/2 inch thick. Cut with 1 1/2-inch round cutter dipped in Bisquick. Place close together around edge of ungreased 2-quart casserole.

3. Spoon turkey mixture into mound in center of biscuits. Bake uncovered 18 to 20 minutes or until biscuits are golden brown and turkey mixture is hot.

High Altitude (3500 to 6500 feet): Bake 22 to 24 minutes.
1 Serving: Calories 370 (Calories from Fat 170); Fat 19g (Saturated 5g); Cholesterol 50mg; Sodium 830mg; Carbohydrate 32g (Dietary Fiber 1g); Protein 19g. **% Daily Value:** Vitamin A 4%; Vitamin C 2%; Calcium 16%; Iron 12%. **Diet Exchanges:** 2 Starch, 2 Medium-Fat Meat, 1 1/2 Fat.

Betty's Tip For an extra-special touch, sprinkle this salad with toasted sliced almonds and dried cranberries, and garnish with fresh sage leaves.

Hot Turkey Salad with Sage Biscuits

Crispy Baked Fish with Tropical Fruit Salsa

4 servings

Tropical Fruit Salsa (below)

3 tablespoons margarine or butter

2/3 cup Original Bisquick

1/4 cup yellow cornmeal

1 teaspoon chili powder

1 1/4 teaspoons salt

1 pound orange roughy fillets or
other white fish fillets

1 egg, beaten

1. Make Tropical Fruit Salsa. Heat oven to 425°. Melt margarine in rectangular pan, 13 x 9 x 2 inches, in oven.

2. Mix Bisquick, cornmeal, chili powder and salt. Dip fish into egg, then coat with Bisquick mixture. Place in pan.

3. Bake uncovered 10 minutes; turn fish. Bake about 15 minutes longer or until fish flakes easily with fork. Serve with salsa.

Tropical Fruit Salsa

1 cup pineapple chunks

1 tablespoon finely chopped red onion

1 tablespoon chopped fresh cilantro

2 tablespoons lime juice

2 kiwifruit, peeled and chopped

1 mango, cut lengthwise in half, pitted and chopped

1 papaya, peeled, seeded and chopped

1 jalapeño chili, seeded and finely chopped

Mix all ingredients in glass or plastic bowl. Cover and refrigerate at least 1 hour to blend flavors.

High Altitude (3500 to 6500 feet): No changes.
1 Serving: Calories 400 (Calories from Fat 110); Fat 12g (Saturated 2g); Cholesterol 100mg; Sodium 1070mg; Carbohydrate 51g (Dietary Fiber 5g); Protein 27g. **% Daily Value:** Vitamin A 46%; Vitamin C 100%; Calcium 10%; Iron 10%. **Diet Exchanges:** 1 Starch, 3 1/2 Very Lean Meat, 2 Fruit, 2 Fat.

Betty's Tip Take a trip to the tropics by serving this dish with couscous or rice that has been cooked in canned coconut milk instead of water.

Crispy Baked Fish with Tropical Fruit Salsa

Tuna Melt Calzone with Cheddar Cheese Sauce

5 servings

1 can (6 ounces) tuna in water, drained

1/2 cup shredded Cheddar cheese (2 ounces)

1 small tomato, chopped (1/2 cup)

1 small onion, chopped (1/4 cup)

1/4 cup chopped celery

3 cups Original Bisquick

1/2 cup water

2 tablespoons vegetable oil

2 tablespoons milk

Cheddar Cheese Sauce (below)

1. Heat oven to 450°. Mix tuna, cheese, tomato, onion and celery; set aside.

2. Stir Bisquick, water and oil until dough forms. Place dough on surface sprinkled with Bisquick; roll in Bisquick to coat. Shape into a ball; knead about 10 times or until smooth. Roll or pat dough into 12-inch circle. Place circle on ungreased cookie sheet. Top half of circle with tuna mixture to within 1 inch of edge. Fold dough over filling; press edge with fork to seal. Brush with milk.

3. Bake 15 to 20 minutes or until golden brown. Immediately remove from cookie sheet to wire rack; cool 5 minutes. Make Cheddar Cheese Sauce. Cut calzone into 5 wedges. Serve with sauce.

Cheddar Cheese Sauce

2 tablespoons margarine or butter

2 tablespoons Original Bisquick

1/4 teaspoon salt

1/8 teaspoon pepper

1 cup milk

3/4 cup shredded sharp Cheddar cheese (3 ounces)

1/4 teaspoon ground mustard

1/8 teaspoon red pepper sauce

Melt margarine in 1-quart saucepan over low heat. Stir in Bisquick, salt and pepper. Cook over low heat, stirring constantly, until mixture is smooth and bubbly. Stir in milk. Heat to boiling, stirring constantly. Boil and stir 1 minute; reduce heat. Stir in cheese, mustard and pepper sauce. Cook until cheese is melted.

High Altitude (3500 to 6500 feet): No changes.
1 Serving: Calories 570 (Calories from Fat 280); Fat 31g (Saturated 11g); Cholesterol 45mg; Sodium 1570mg; Carbohydrate 51g (Dietary Fiber 1g); Protein 23g. **% Daily Value:** Vitamin A 16%; Vitamin C 4%; Calcium 34%; Iron 18%. **Diet Exchanges:** 3 Starch, 2 Lean Meat, 1 Vegetable, 4 1/2 Fat.

Tuna Melt Calzone with Cheddar Cheese Sauce

Southwestern Bean Bake

6 servings

1 can (15 to 16 ounces) kidney beans, rinsed and drained

1 can (15 to 16 ounces) great northern beans, rinsed and drained

1 can (14 1/2 ounces) stewed tomatoes, undrained

1/2 cup salsa

1/4 cup ketchup

1 1/2 cups Original Bisquick

1/2 cup yellow cornmeal

2/3 cup milk

1 tablespoon margarine or butter, softened

4 medium green onions, sliced (1/4 cup)

1. Heat oven to 425°. Heat beans, tomatoes, salsa and ketchup to boiling in 2-quart saucepan, stirring occasionally; remove from heat. Pour into ungreased 2-quart casserole.

2. Stir remaining ingredients until soft dough forms; beat 20 strokes. Drop dough by spoonfuls onto bean mixture; spread to edge of casserole.

3. Bake uncovered 20 to 25 minutes or until golden brown.

High Altitude (3500 to 6500 feet): No changes.
1 Serving: Calories 400 (Calories from Fat 70); Fat 8g (Saturated 3g); Cholesterol 5mg; Sodium 1000mg; Carbohydrate 73g (Dietary Fiber 10g); Protein 19g. **% Daily Value:** Vitamin A 8%; Vitamin C 14%; Calcium 20%; Iron 38%. **Diet Exchanges:** 4 Starch, 1/2 Lean Meat, 2 Vegetable.

Betty's Tip Make a weekday Southwest fiesta by serving this tasty dish with a side of fiery salsa, sour cream and chopped green chilies.

Southwestern Bean Bake

Extra-Easy Veggie Pizza

8 servings

1 1/2 cups Original Bisquick

1/3 cup very hot water

1 can (8 ounces) pizza sauce

1/2 cup sliced mushrooms

1 large bell pepper, chopped (1 cup)

1 small red onion, sliced and separated into rings

1 1/2 cups shredded mozzarella cheese (6 ounces)

1. Heat oven to 450°. Grease 12-inch pizza pan. Stir Bisquick and hot water; beat 20 strokes until soft dough forms. Press dough in pizza pan, using fingers dusted with Bisquick; pinch edge to form 1/2-inch rim.

2. Spread pizza sauce over dough. Top with mushrooms, bell pepper and onion. Sprinkle with cheese.

3. Bake 12 to 15 minutes or until crust is golden brown and cheese is melted.

High Altitude (3500 to 6500 feet): No changes.
1 Serving: Calories 225 (Calories from Fat 115); Fat 13g (Saturated 5g); Cholesterol 20mg; Sodium 780mg; Carbohydrate 18g (Dietary Fiber 1g); Protein 10g. **% Daily Value:** Vitamin A 6%; Vitamin C 12%; Calcium 20%; Iron 6%. **Diet Exchanges:** 1 Starch, 1 High-Fat Meat, 1 Fat.

Bisquick really delivers in the 1980s—great pizza, pronto!

Extra-Easy Veggie Pizza

Asian Oven Pancake

4 servings

1/3 cup water

2 tablespoons margarine or butter

1/2 cup Original Bisquick

2 eggs

1 tablespoon vegetable oil

1 medium stalk celery, cut into
  1/4-inch diagonal slices (1/2 cup)

1 medium carrot, thinly sliced
  (1/2 cup)

1/3 cup red bell pepper strips

1/2 cup bean sprouts

1/3 cup sliced mushrooms

2 medium green onions, thinly
  sliced (2 tablespoons)

1 can (8 ounces) bamboo shoots,
  drained

1 clove garlic, finely chopped

1/4 cup teriyaki baste and glaze
  (from 12-ounce bottle)

1/4 cup cashew halves

1. Heat oven to 400°. Generously grease pie plate, 9 x 1 1/4 inches. Heat water and margarine to boiling in 1-quart saucepan; reduce heat to low. Add Bisquick all at once. Stir vigorously over low heat about 1 minute or until mixture forms a ball; remove from heat.

2. Beat in eggs, one at a time, using spoon; beat until smooth and glossy. Spread in pie plate (do not spread up sides). Bake 20 to 25 minutes or until puffed and dry in center.

3. While pancake is baking, heat oil in 10-inch skillet over medium-high heat. Cook celery, carrot and bell pepper in oil 2 minutes, stirring occasionally. Stir in bean sprouts, mushrooms, onions, bamboo shoots and garlic. Cook 1 to 2 minutes, stirring occasionally, until mushrooms are tender. Stir in teriyaki glaze; cook 2 minutes. Spoon over hot pancake. Sprinkle with cashews. Cut into four wedges. Serve immediately.

High Altitude (3500 to 6500 feet): No changes.
1 Serving: Calories 220 (Calories from Fat 130); Fat 14g (Saturated 6g); Cholesterol 120mg; Sodium 1000mg; Carbohydrate 18g (Dietary Fiber 2g); Protein 8g. **% Daily Value:** Vitamin A 32%; Vitamin C 12%; Calcium 8%; Iron 8%. **Diet Exchanges:** 1 Starch; 1 Vegetable, 2 Fat.

Betty's Tip Bottled teriyaki sauces vary from brand to brand. Some are thick, and others are much thinner. We recommend using teriyaki baste and glaze. It's thicker than the sauces and coats the vegetables nicely.

Asian Oven Pancake

Wild Rice Soup

5 servings

2 tablespoons margarine or butter

2 medium stalks celery, sliced
(1 cup)

1 medium carrot, coarsely shredded
(1 cup)

1 medium onion, chopped (1/2 cup)

1 small green bell pepper, chopped
(1/2 cup)

1/4 cup Original Bisquick

1/2 teaspoon salt

1/4 teaspoon pepper

1 cup water

1 can (10 1/2 ounces) condensed
chicken broth

1 1/2 cups cooked wild rice

1 cup half-and-half

1/3 cup slivered almonds, toasted
(page 18)

1/4 cup chopped fresh parsley

1. Melt margarine in 3-quart saucepan over medium-high heat. Cook celery, carrot, onion and bell pepper in margarine about 4 minutes, stirring occasionally, until tender.

2. Stir in Bisquick, salt and pepper. Stir in water, broth and wild rice. Heat to boiling, stirring frequently; reduce heat to low. Cover and simmer 15 minutes, stirring occasionally.

3. Stir in half-and-half, almonds and parsley. Heat just until hot (do not boil).

High Altitude (3500 to 6500 feet): No changes.
1 Serving: Calories 260 (Calories from Fat 145); Fat 16g (Saturated 5g); Cholesterol 20mg; Sodium 700mg; Carbohydrate 24g (Dietary Fiber 3g); Protein 8g. **%Daily Value:** Vitamin A 32%; Vitamin C 24%; Calcium 10%; Iron 8%. **Diet Exchanges:** 1 Starch, 2 Vegetable, 3 Fat

Betty's Tip   Purchase canned wild rice to save on prep time. A 15-ounce can contains about 2 cups cooked wild rice.

Wild Rice Soup

impossibly easy
pies

Impossibly Easy Coconut Pie (page 162), Impossibly Easy Taco Pie (page 163)

Impossibly Easy Coconut Pie
8 servings

1 cup flaked or shredded coconut

3/4 cup sugar

1/2 cup Original Bisquick

1/4 cup margarine or butter, softened

2 cups milk

1 1/2 teaspoons vanilla

4 eggs

Whipped topping, if desired

Papaya or mango slices, if desired

1. Heat oven to 350°. Grease pie plate, 9 x 1 1/4 inches.
2. Stir all ingredients, except whipped topping and papaya, until blended. Pour into pie plate.
3. Bake 50 to 55 minutes or knife inserted in center comes out clean. Cool 5 minutes. Garnish with whipped topping and papaya. Store covered in refrigerator.

High Altitude (3500 to 6500 feet): Bake about 55 minutes.
1 Serving: Calories 270 (Calories from Fat 125); Fat 14g (Saturated 6g); Cholesterol 110mg; Sodium 270mg; Carbohydrate 31g (Dietary Fiber 1g); Protein 6g. **% Daily Value:** Vitamin A 14%; Vitamin C 0%; Calcium 10%; Iron 4%. **Diet Exchanges:** 2 Starch, 2 1/2 Fat.

Betty's Tip Did you know that Impossible Coconut Pie was the very first Impossible Pie in the 1960s? It was so popular that a whole family of what we now call Impossibly Easy Pies was born. Mix all the ingredients together, and pour into a pie plate. While it bakes, the crust is formed—easier than pie!

Impossibly Easy Taco Pie
6 servings

1 pound ground beef

1 medium onion, chopped (1/2 cup)

1 envelope (1 1/4 ounces) taco seasoning mix

1 can (4 ounces) chopped green chilies, drained

1/2 cup Original Bisquick

1 cup milk

2 eggs

3/4 cup shredded Monterey Jack or Cheddar cheese (3 ounces)

Salsa, if desired

Sour cream, if desired

1. Heat oven to 400°. Grease pie plate, 9 x 1 1/4 inches. Cook beef and onion in 10-inch skillet over medium heat, stirring occasionally, until beef is brown; drain. Stir in seasoning mix (dry). Spread in pie plate. Top with chilies.

2. Stir Bisquick, milk and eggs until blended. Pour into pie plate.

3. Bake about 25 minutes or until knife inserted in center comes out clean. Sprinkle with cheese. Bake 2 to 3 minutes or until cheese is melted. Let stand 5 minutes before serving. Serve with salsa and sour cream.

High Altitude (3500 to 6500 feet): Increase first bake time to about 28 minutes.
1 Serving: Calories 315 (Calories from Fat 170); Fat 19g (Saturated 8g); Cholesterol 130mg; Sodium 590mg; Carbohydrate 15g (Dietary Fiber 1g); Protein 22g. **% Daily Value:** Vitamin A 16%; Vitamin C 14%; Calcium 20%; Iron 12%. **Diet Exchanges:** 1 Starch, 3 Medium-Fat Meat.

Betty's Tip In addition to the salsa and sour cream, try serving this zesty pie with shredded lettuce, chopped jalapeño chilies and sliced green onions.

Impossibly Easy Lasagna Pie

6 servings

1 pound ground beef

1/2 cup thick-and-chunky tomato pasta sauce

1/3 cup ricotta cheese

3 tablespoons grated Parmesan cheese

1 tablespoon milk

1/2 teaspoon salt

1 cup shredded mozzarella cheese (4 ounces)

1/2 cup Original Bisquick

1 cup milk

2 eggs

1. Heat oven to 400°. Grease pie plate, 9 x 1 1/4 inches. Cook beef in 10-inch skillet over medium heat, stirring occasionally, until brown; drain. Stir in pasta sauce; heat until bubbly.

2. Mix ricotta cheese, Parmesan cheese, 1 tablespoon milk and the salt. Spread half of the beef mixture in pie plate. Drop cheese mixture by spoonfuls onto beef mixture. Sprinkle with 1/2 cup of the mozzarella cheese. Top with remaining beef mixture. Stir Bisquick, 1 cup milk and the eggs until blended. Pour into pie plate.

3. Bake 30 to 35 minutes or until knife inserted in center comes out clean. Sprinkle with remaining 1/2 cup mozzarella cheese. Bake 2 to 3 minutes or until cheese is melted. Let stand 5 minutes before serving.

High Altitude (3500 to 6500 feet): Heat oven to 425°.
1 Serving: Calories 350 (Calories from Fat 190); Fat 21g (Saturated 9g); Cholesterol 135mg; Sodium 680mg; Carbohydrate 14g (Dietary Fiber 0g); Protein 26g. **% Daily Value:** Vitamin A 10%; Vitamin C 2%; Calcium 30%; Iron 10%. **Diet Exchanges:** 1 Starch, 1 Medium-Fat Meat, 1 Fat.

Trust Bisquick to outdo itself—this 1980s ad shows this recipe easier to make than pie. Everything should be this simple.

Impossibly Easy Lasagna Pie

Impossibly Easy Pizza Pie
6 servings

1 medium onion, chopped (1/2 cup)

1/3 cup grated Parmesan cheese

1/2 cup Original Bisquick

1 cup milk

2 eggs

1 can (8 ounces) pizza sauce

1/2 package (3-ounce size) sliced pepperoni

1/4 cup chopped green bell pepper

3/4 cup shredded mozzarella cheese (3 ounces)

1. Heat oven to 400°. Grease pie plate, 9 x 1 1/4 inches. Sprinkle onion and Parmesan cheese in pie plate.

2. Stir Bisquick, milk and eggs until blended. Pour into pie plate.

3. Bake 20 minutes. Spread with pizza sauce; top with remaining ingredients. Bake 10 to 15 minutes or until cheese is light brown. Let stand 5 minutes before serving. Sprinkle with additional Parmesan cheese if desired.

High Altitude (3500 to 6500 feet): Increase first bake time to 33 minutes.
1 Serving: Calories 215 (Calories from Fat 115); Fat 13g (Saturated 6g); Cholesterol 95mg; Sodium 650mg; Carbohydrate 14g (Dietary Fiber 1g); Protein 12g. **% Daily Value:** Vitamin A 10%; Vitamin C 14%; Calcium 24%; Iron 6%. **Diet Exchanges:** 1 Starch, 1 1/2 Medium-Fat Meat, 1/2 Fat.

Betty's Tip Doubling any Impossibly Easy Pie recipe is a breeze. Just double the ingredients, and bake in either two pie plates, 9 x 1 1/4 inches each, or in a 13 x 9 x 2-inch baking dish. If you use the baking dish, bake the pie for 10 minutes longer than the recipe indicates.

Impossibly Easy Pizza Pie

Impossibly Easy Ham and Swiss Pie

6 servings

1 1/2 cups cut-up fully cooked ham

1 cup shredded Swiss cheese
   (4 ounces)

4 medium green onions, sliced
   (1/4 cup)

1/2 cup Original Bisquick

1 cup milk

1/4 teaspoon salt

1/8 teaspoon pepper

2 eggs

1. Heat oven to 400°. Grease pie plate, 9 x 1 1/4 inches. Sprinkle ham, cheese and onions in pie plate.

2. Stir remaining ingredients until blended. Pour into pie plate.

3. Bake 35 to 40 minutes or until knife inserted in center comes out clean. Let stand 5 minutes before serving.

High Altitude (3500 to 6500 feet): Bake about 45 minutes.
1 Serving: Calories 215 (Calories from Fat 110); Fat 12g (Saturated 6g); Cholesterol 110mg; Sodium 830mg; Carbohydrate 10g (Dietary Fiber 0g); Protein 17g. **% Daily Value:** Vitamin A 8%; Vitamin C 2%; Calcium 26%; Iron 6%. **Diet Exchanges:** 1/2 Starch, 2 Lean Meat, 1 Fat.

Betty's Tip Impossibly Easy Pies are as easy to reheat as they are to make. To reheat in the microwave, arrange slices evenly spaced and with points toward the center on a large microwavable plate. Cover with waxed paper (except those with a cheese topping) and microwave on Medium 2 to 3 minutes per slice. Rotate 1/2 turn after 3 minutes. Let stand 2 minutes before serving.

Impossibly Easy Ham and Swiss Pie

Impossibly Easy Chicken and Broccoli Pie

6 servings

1 package (10 ounces) frozen chopped broccoli, thawed and drained

1 1/2 cups shredded Cheddar cheese (6 ounces)

1 cup cut-up cooked chicken

1 medium onion, chopped (1/2 cup)

1/2 cup Original Bisquick

1 cup milk

1/2 teaspoon salt

1/4 teaspoon pepper

2 eggs

1. Heat oven to 400°. Grease pie plate, 9 x 1 1/4 inches. Sprinkle broccoli, 1 cup of the cheese, the chicken and onion in pie plate.

2. Stir remaining ingredients until blended. Pour into pie plate.

3. Bake 30 to 35 minutes or until knife inserted in center comes out clean. Sprinkle with remaining 1/2 cup cheese. Bake 1 to 2 minutes or until cheese is melted. Let stand 5 minutes before serving.

High Altitude (3500 to 6500 feet): Heat oven to 425°. Increase first bake time to 33 to 38 minutes.

1 Serving: Calories 260 (Calories from Fat 145); Fat 16g (Saturated 8g); Cholesterol 125mg; Sodium 580mg; Carbohydrate 12g (Dietary Fiber 2g); Protein 19g. **% Daily Value:** Vitamin A 18%; Vitamin C 14%; Calcium 24%; Iron 6%. **Diet Exchanges:** 1/2 Starch, 2 Lean Meat, 1 Vegetable, 2 Fat.

Pull up a chair—whether it's the 1960s or tonight, you're always prepared with Bisquick!

Impossibly Easy Chicken and Broccoli Pie

Impossibly Easy Chicken Primavera Pie

6 servings

1 1/2 cups cut-up cooked chicken

1 package (10 ounces) frozen asparagus cuts, thawed and well drained

1 cup frozen stir-fry bell peppers and onions (from 16-ounce bag), thawed and well drained

1/3 cup grated Parmesan cheese

1/2 cup Original Bisquick

1 cup milk

1/2 teaspoon salt

2 eggs

1. Heat oven to 400°. Grease pie plate, 9 x 1 1/4 inches. Layer chicken, asparagus, stir-fry mixture and cheese in pie plate.

2. Stir remaining ingredients until blended. Pour into pie plate.

3. Bake 30 to 35 minutes or until knife inserted in center comes out clean. Let stand 5 minutes before serving.

High Altitude (3500 to 6500 feet): Bake 38 to 40 minutes.
1 Serving: Calories 185 (Calories from Fat 70); Fat 8g (Saturated 3g); Cholesterol 105mg; Sodium 490mg; Carbohydrate 12g (Dietary Fiber 1g); Protein 17g. **% Daily Value:** Vitamin A 8%; Vitamin C 14%; Calcium 14%; Iron 8%. **Diet Exchanges:** 1/2 Starch, 2 Lean Meat, 1 Vegetable.

Betty's Tip Is company coming? Garnish each serving of this pie with a spoonful of warmed marinara or spaghetti sauce and a sprinkle of freshly shredded Parmesan cheese on top.

Impossibly Easy Chicken Primavera Pie

Impossibly Easy Salmon-Asparagus Pie

8 servings

1 pound asparagus, cut into 1-inch pieces (2 cups)

4 medium green onions, sliced (1/4 cup)

1 1/2 cups shredded Swiss cheese (6 ounces)

1 can (6 ounces) skinless boneless pink salmon, drained and flaked

1/2 cup Original Bisquick

1 cup milk

1 1/2 teaspoons chopped fresh or 1/2 teaspoon dried basil leaves

1/8 teaspoon pepper

2 eggs

1. Heat oven to 400°. Grease pie plate, 9 x 1 1/4 inches. Sprinkle asparagus, onions, 3/4 cup of the cheese and the salmon in pie plate.

2. Stir remaining ingredients until blended. Pour into pie plate.

3. Bake 30 to 35 minutes or until knife inserted in center comes out clean. Immediately sprinkle with remaining 3/4 cup cheese. Bake about 2 minutes or until cheese is melted. Let stand 10 minutes before serving.

High Altitude (3500 to 6500 feet): Increase first bake time to 50 to 55 minutes.
1 Serving: Calories 175 (Calories from fat 90); Fat 10g (Saturated 5g); Cholesterol 85mg; Sodium 310mg; Carbohydrate 8g (Dietary Fiber 1g); Protein 14g. **% Daily Value:** Vitamin A 8%; Vitamin C 6%; Calcium 30%; Iron 4%. **Diet Exchanges:** 1 1/2 Lean Meat, 2 Vegetable, 1 Fat.

Betty's Tip Here's a simple substitution: Use 1 package (10 ounces) frozen cut asparagus, thawed and well drained, instead of the fresh asparagus. Decrease the milk from 1 cup to 3/4 cup, and increase the Bisquick from 1/2 cup to 3/4 cup.

Impossibly Easy Salmon-Asparagus Pie

Impossibly Easy Mac 'n' Cheese Pie

6 servings

1 cup uncooked elbow macaroni
(3 1/2 ounces)

2 cups shredded Cheddar cheese
(8 ounces)

1/2 cup Original Bisquick

1 1/2 cups milk

1/4 teaspoon red pepper sauce

2 eggs

1. Heat oven to 400°. Grease pie plate, 9 x 1 1/4 inches. Place uncooked macaroni in pie plate. Sprinkle with 1 3/4 cups of the cheese.

2. Stir remaining ingredients until blended. Pour into pie plate.

3. Bake 25 to 30 minutes or until knife inserted in center comes out clean. Sprinkle with remaining 1/4 cup cheese. Bake 1 to 2 minutes or until cheese is melted. Let stand 5 minutes before serving.

High Altitude (3500 to 6500 feet): Cook macaroni in boiling water 5 minutes (add 1 tablespoon vegetable oil to prevent boilover). Drain thoroughly; cool completely.
1 Serving: Calories 320 (Calories from Fat 155); Fat 17g (Saturated 10g); Cholesterol 115mg; Sodium 430mg; Carbohydrate 26g (Dietary Fiber 1g); Protein 17g. **% Daily Value:** Vitamin A 12%; Vitamin C 0%; Calcium 30%; Iron 8%. **Diet Exchanges:** 2 Starch, 1 1/2 Medium-Fat Meat, 1 Fat.

Betty's Tip Add some color to this comfort-food classic with a dash of paprika and a little chopped fresh parsley. If you're craving something crunchy, sprinkle crushed seasoned croutons over the top.

Impossibly Easy Mac 'n' Cheese Pie

Impossibly Easy Spinach Pie

6 servings

1 tablespoon margarine or butter

8 medium green onions, sliced (1/2 cup)

2 cloves garlic, finely chopped

1 package (10 ounces) frozen chopped spinach, thawed and squeezed to drain

1/2 cup small curd creamed cottage cheese

1/2 cup Original Bisquick

1 cup milk

1 teaspoon lemon juice

1/4 teaspoon pepper

3 eggs

3 tablespoons grated Parmesan cheese

1/4 teaspoon ground nutmeg

1. Heat oven to 350°. Grease pie plate, 9 x 1 1/4 inches. Melt margarine in 10-inch skillet over medium heat. Cook onions and garlic in margarine 2 to 3 minutes, stirring occasionally, until onions are tender. Stir in spinach. Layer spinach mixture and cottage cheese in pie plate.

2. Stir Bisquick, milk, lemon juice, pepper and eggs until blended. Pour into pie plate. Sprinkle with Parmesan cheese and nutmeg.

3. Bake about 35 minutes or until knife inserted in center comes out clean. Let stand 5 minutes before serving. Sprinkle with additional sliced green onions if desired.

High Altitude (3500 to 6500 feet): Bake 35 to 40 minutes.
1 Serving: Calories 150 (Calories from Fat 70); Fat 8g (Saturated 3g); Cholesterol 115mg; Sodium 360mg; Carbohydrate 11g (Dietary Fiber 1g); Protein 10g. **% Daily Value:** Vitamin A 32%; Vitamin C 4%; Calcium 18%; Iron 6%. **Diet Exchanges:** 1 Lean Meat, 2 Vegetable, 1 Fat.

Betty's Tip In search of a speedy spinach tip? To quickly thaw spinach, place it in a colander or strainer and rinse with warm water until thawed. Squeeze dry with paper towels.

Impossibly Easy Spinach Pie, Impossibly Easy Zucchini Pie (page 180)

Impossibly Easy Zucchini Pie

6 servings

1 small zucchini, chopped (1 cup)

1 large tomato, chopped (1 cup)

1 medium onion, chopped (1/2 cup)

1/3 cup grated Parmesan cheese

1/2 cup Original Bisquick

1 cup milk

1/2 teaspoon salt

1/8 teaspoon pepper

2 eggs

1. Heat oven to 400°. Grease pie plate, 9 x 1 1/4 inches. Layer zucchini, tomato, onion and cheese in pie plate.

2. Stir remaining ingredients until blended. Pour into pie plate.

3. Bake about 35 minutes or until knife inserted in center comes out clean. Let stand 5 minutes before serving.

High Altitude (3500 to 6500 feet): Use 3/4 cup Bisquick. Bake 35 to 40 minutes.
1 Serving: Calories 115 (Calories from Fat 45); Fat 5g (Saturated 2g); Cholesterol 75mg; Sodium 470mg; Carbohydrate 12g (Dietary Fiber 1g); Protein 7g. **% Daily Value:** Vitamin A 8%; Vitamin C 6%; Calcium 14%; Iron 4%. **Diet Exchanges:** 1/2 Starch, 1/2 High-Fat Meat, 1 Vegetable.

Betty's Tip Blessed with a bumper crop of zucchini? Store zucchini and other summer squash in a plastic bag in the refrigerator for up to five days.

Impossibly Easy Cheesecake

8 servings

3/4 cup milk

2 teaspoons vanilla

2 eggs

1 cup sugar

1/2 cup Original Bisquick

2 packages (8 ounces each) cream cheese, cut into about 1/2-inch cubes and softened

Sour Cream Topping (below)

Fresh raspberries, if desired

Kiwifruit slices, if desired

1. Heat oven to 350°. Grease pie plate, 9 x 1 1/4 inches.

2. Place milk, vanilla, eggs, sugar and Bisquick in blender. Cover and blend on high speed 15 seconds. Add cream cheese. Blend 2 minutes. Pour into pie plate.

3. Bake uncovered 40 to 45 minutes or until knife inserted in center comes out clean. Cool completely, about 1 hour. Spread Sour Cream Topping over top of cooled cheesecake. Refrigerate until ready to serve. Top with raspberries and kiwifruit. Store covered in refrigerator.

Sour Cream Topping

1 cup sour cream

2 tablespoons sugar

2 teaspoons vanilla

Stir all ingredients until blended.

High Altitude (3500 to 6500 feet): Bake 45 to 50 minutes.
1 Serving: Calories 430 (Calories from Fat 250); Fat 28g (Saturated 17g); Cholesterol 135mg; Sodium 310mg; Carbohydrate 37g (Dietary Fiber 0g); Protein 8g. **% Daily Value:** Vitamin A 24%; Vitamin C 0%; Calcium 12%; Iron 6%. **Diet Exchanges:** Not Recommended.

Betty's Tip For a deliciously decadent cheesecake, omit the Sour Cream Topping, and instead, drizzle with fudge and caramel toppings and sprinkle with chopped pecans.

Impossibly Easy Mocha Fudge Cheesecake

8 servings

1 tablespoon instant coffee (dry)

3 tablespoons coffee liqueur or strong brewed coffee, cooled to room temperature

2 packages (8 ounces each) cream cheese, softened

3/4 cup Original Bisquick

3/4 cup sugar

1 teaspoon vanilla

3 eggs

3 ounces semisweet baking chocolate, melted and cooled

Chocolate Topping (below)

1. Heat oven to 350°. Grease pie plate, 9 x 1 1/4 inches. Stir coffee and liqueur until coffee is dissolved.

2. Beat coffee mixture and remaining ingredients except Chocolate Topping in large bowl with electric mixer on high speed about 2 minutes, scraping bowl frequently, until well blended. Pour into pie plate.

3. Bake about 35 minutes or until center is firm and puffed. Cool 5 minutes (top of cheesecake will be cracked). Carefully spread Chocolate Topping over cheesecake. Refrigerate at least 3 hours before serving. Store covered in refrigerator.

Chocolate Topping

1 ounce semisweet baking chocolate, melted and cooled

2 tablespoons powdered sugar

1 tablespoon coffee liqueur, if desired

1 container (8 ounces) sour cream

1 teaspoon vanilla

Stir chocolate, powdered sugar and liqueur in small bowl until blended. Stir in sour cream and vanilla.

High Altitude (3500 to 6500 feet): Bake about 40 minutes.
1 Serving: Calories 490 (Calories from Fat 295); Fat 33g (Saturated 19g); Cholesterol 160mg; Sodium 360mg; Carbohydrate 40g (Dietary Fiber 1g); Protein 9g. **% Daily Value:** Vitamin A 24%; Vitamin C 0%; Calcium 10%; Iron 10%. **Diet Exchanges:** Not Recommended.

Betty's Tip Dress up this chocolate-lover's cheesecake with a few chocolate curls, a drizzle of raspberry sauce or a dusting of powdered sugar.

Impossibly Easy Cheesecake (page 181), Impossibly Easy Mocha Fudge Cheesecake

Impossibly Easy French Apple Pie

8 servings

Streusel Topping (below)

3 large all-purpose apples
  (Braeburn, Gala or Haralson),
  peeled and thinly sliced (3 cups)

1/2 cup Original Bisquick

1/2 cup sugar

1/2 cup milk

1 tablespoon margarine or butter,
  softened

1 teaspoon ground cinnamon

1/4 teaspoon ground nutmeg

2 eggs

1. Heat oven to 350°. Grease pie plate, 9 x 1 1/4 inches. Make Streusel Topping; set aside. Spread apples in pie plate.

2. In separate bowl, stir remaining ingredients until blended. Pour over apples. Sprinkle with topping.

3. Bake 40 to 45 minutes or until knife inserted in center comes out clean. Cool 5 minutes.

Streusel Topping

1/2 cup Original Bisquick

1/4 cup chopped nuts

1/4 cup packed brown sugar

2 tablespoons firm margarine or butter

Mix Bisquick, nuts and brown sugar. Cut in margarine, using fork or pastry blender, until mixture is crumbly.

High Altitude (3500 to 6500 feet): Heat oven to 375°.
1 Serving: Calories 235 (Calories from Fat 90); Fat 10g (Saturated 2g); Cholesterol 55mg; Sodium 290mg; Carbohydrate 33g (Dietary Fiber 1g); Protein 4g. **% Daily Value:** Vitamin A 8%; Vitamin C 0%; Calcium 6%; Iron 4%. **Diet Exchanges:** 1 Starch, 1 Fruit, 2 Fat.

Betty's Tip To make **Impossibly Easy Peach Pie,** substitute 2 cans (16 ounces each) sliced peaches, well drained, or 4 medium peaches, peeled and sliced (3 cups) for the apples.

Impossibly Easy French Apple Pie

Impossibly Easy Cherry-Almond Pie

8 servings

1/2 cup Original Bisquick

1/4 cup sugar

3/4 cup milk

2 tablespoons margarine or butter, softened

1/4 teaspoon almond extract

2 eggs

1 can (21 ounces) cherry pie filling

Brown Sugar Streusel (below)

Slivered almonds, toasted (page 18), if desired

1. Heat oven to 400°. Grease pie plate, 9 x 1 1/4 inches.

2. Stir all ingredients except pie filling, Brown Sugar Streusel and almonds until blended. Pour into pie plate. Spoon pie filling over top.

3. Bake 30 minutes. Sprinkle Brown Sugar Streusel over pie filling. Bake about 10 minutes or until streusel is golden brown; cool. Sprinkle with almonds.

Brown Sugar Streusel

1/2 cup Original Bisquick

1/2 cup packed brown sugar

1/2 teaspoon ground cinnamon

2 tablespoons firm margarine or butter

Mix Bisquick, brown sugar and cinnamon. Cut in margarine, using fork or pastry blender, until mixture is crumbly.

High Altitude (3500 to 6500 feet): Increase second bake time to 15 to 20 minutes.
1 Serving: Calories 295 (Calories from fat 90); Fat 10g (Saturated 5g); Cholesterol 70mg; Sodium 290mg; Carbohydrate 48g (Dietary Fiber 1g); Protein 4g. **% Daily Value:** Vitamin A 8%; Vitamin C 0%; Calcium 8%; Iron 6%. **Diet Exchanges:** 1 Starch, 2 Fruit, 2 Fat.

Betty's Tip Stick with the stick! The streusel topping will blend better and be more crumbly if you use margarine or butter from a stick instead of a soft spread.

Impossibly Easy Cherry-Almond Pie

Impossibly Easy Pumpkin-Pecan Pie

8 servings

1 cup canned pumpkin
  (not pumpkin pie mix)

1 cup evaporated milk

1/2 cup Original Bisquick

1/2 cup sugar

1 tablespoon margarine or butter,
  softened

1 1/2 teaspoons pumpkin pie spice

1 teaspoon vanilla

2 eggs

1/2 cup chopped pecans

Spiced Topping (below)

8 pecan halves, if desired

1. Heat oven to 350°. Grease pie plate, 9 x 1 1/4 inches.

2. Stir all ingredients except pecans and Spiced Topping until blended. Stir in chopped pecans. Pour into pie plate.

3. Bake 35 to 40 minutes or until knife inserted in center comes out clean. Cool completely, about 1 hour. Cut pie into slices. Garnish each serving with Spiced Topping and pecan. Store covered in refrigerator.

Spiced Topping

1 1/2 cups frozen (thawed) whipped topping

1/4 teaspoon pumpkin pie spice

Stir ingredients until smooth.

High Altitude (3500 to 6500 feet): Heat oven to 375°.
1 Serving: Calories 225 (Calories from fat 110); Fat 12g (Saturated 4g); Cholesterol 60mg; Sodium 180mg; Carbohydrate 26g (Dietary Fiber 2g); Protein 5g. **% Daily Value:** Vitamin A 74%; Vitamin C 0%; Calcium 12%; Iron 6%. **Diet Exchanges:** 1 Starch, 2 Vegetable, 2 Fat.

Nothing's Impossible with Bisquick! This 1981 ad gives everyone a headstart on the holidays by slashing stress, and best of all, by recommending a truly delicious pie.

Impossibly Easy Pumpkin-Pecan Pie

Impossibly Easy Banana Custard Pie

8 servings

1 cup mashed ripe bananas
(2 medium)

2 teaspoons lemon juice

1/2 cup Original Bisquick

1/4 cup sugar

1 tablespoon margarine or butter,
softened

1/2 teaspoon vanilla

2 eggs

1 can (14 ounces) sweetened
condensed milk

3/4 cup frozen (thawed) whipped
topping

1/4 cup coarsely chopped walnuts,
if desired

Caramel topping, warmed,
if desired

1. Heat oven to 350°. Grease pie plate, 9 x 1 1/4 inches. Mix bananas and lemon juice; set aside.

2. Stir remaining ingredients except whipped topping and walnuts in medium bowl until blended. Add banana mixture; stir until blended. Pour into pie plate.

3. Bake 40 to 45 minutes or until golden brown and knife inserted in center comes out clean; cool. Cover and refrigerate about 2 hours or until chilled. Spread with whipped topping; sprinkle with walnuts. Drizzle with caramel topping. Store covered in refrigerator.

High Altitude (3500 to 6500 feet): No changes.
1 Serving: Calories 345 (Calories from Fat 100); Fat 11g (Saturated 5g); Cholesterol 75mg; Sodium 230mg; Carbohydrate 55g (Dietary Fiber 1g); Protein 8g. **% Daily Value:** Vitamin A 8%; Vitamin C 0%; Calcium 20%; Iron 2%. **Diet Exchanges:** Not Recommended.

Betty's Tip Don't throw away those speckled brown bananas! Their sweet flavor and soft texture are what make this easy pie so delicious.

Impossibly Easy Banana Custard Pie

delicious desserts

Chocolate Swirl Cake (page 194), Neapolitan Shortcake Parfaits (page 195)

Chocolate Swirl Cake

16 servings

3 cups Original Bisquick

3/4 cup sugar

1/4 cup shortening

1 cup cold milk or water

1 tablespoon vanilla

2 eggs

2 ounces semisweet baking
   chocolate, melted and cooled

Chocolate Frosting (below)

1. Heat oven to 350°. Grease and flour rectangular pan, 13 x 9 x 2 inches. Beat all ingredients except chocolate and Chocolate Frosting in large bowl with electric mixer on low speed 30 seconds, scraping bowl constantly. Beat on medium speed 4 minutes, scraping bowl occasionally.

2. Pour 3 cups of the batter into pan. Beat melted chocolate into remaining batter on medium speed until well blended. Drop chocolate batter randomly by tablespoonfuls onto white batter. Swirl knife through batters for swirled design.

3. Bake 30 to 35 minutes or until toothpick inserted in center comes out clean. Cool completely, about 1 hour. Frost with Chocolate Frosting.

Chocolate Frosting

1/3 cup margarine or butter, softened

2 ounces unsweetened baking chocolate, melted and cooled

2 cups powdered sugar

1 1/2 teaspoons vanilla

About 2 tablespoons milk

Stir margarine and chocolate in medium bowl until blended. Stir in remaining ingredients. Beat until smooth and spreadable.

High Altitude (3500 to 6500 feet): Heat oven to 375°. Use 1 cup sugar, 1 1/2 cups milk or water and 3 eggs.

1 Serving: Calories 300 (Calories from Fat 115); Fat 13g (Saturated 4g); Cholesterol 25mg; Sodium 380mg; Carbohydrate 43g (Dietary Fiber 1g); Protein 3g. **% Daily Value:** Vitamin A 6%; Vitamin C 0%; Calcium 4%; Iron 6%. **Diet Exchanges:** Not Recommended.

Betty's Tip Check your chocolate—baking chocolate works best in this recipe. Melted chocolate chips will harden when dropped onto the batter, making it difficult to swirl.

Neapolitan Shortcake Parfaits

8 servings

2 1/3 cups Original Bisquick

1/2 cup milk

3 tablespoons sugar

3 tablespoons margarine or butter, melted

1 bag (6 ounces) semisweet chocolate chips (1 cup)

1 tablespoon shortening

Sweetened Whipped Cream (below)

1 quart (4 cups) strawberries, cut up

1. Heat oven to 425°. Stir Bisquick, milk, sugar and margarine until soft dough forms. Drop dough by 6 spoonfuls onto ungreased cookie sheet. Bake 10 to 12 minutes or until golden brown; cool slightly. Crumble into small pieces.

2. Place chocolate chips and shortening in small microwavable bowl. Microwave uncovered on Medium (50%) 1 to 2 minutes, stirring after 1 minute, until mixture can be stirred smooth and is thin enough to drizzle.

3. Make Sweetened Whipped Cream. For each serving, alternate layers of crumbled shortcake, strawberries, melted chocolate and whipped cream in parfait glasses. Serve immediately.

Sweetened Whipped Cream

1 1/2 cups whipping (heavy) cream

1/3 cup powdered sugar

Beat ingredients in chilled medium bowl with electric mixer on high speed until stiff.

High Altitude (3500 to 6500 feet): Heat oven to 450°. Use 1 tablespoon sugar in shortcakes.
1 Serving: Calories 505 (Calories from Fat 290); Fat 32g (Saturated 15g); Cholesterol 50mg; Sodium 580mg; Carbohydrate 52g (Dietary Fiber 3g); Protein 5g. **% Daily Value:** Vitamin A 16%; Vitamin C 72%; Calcium 12%; Iron 10%. **Diet Exchanges:** Not Recommended.

In 1942, Bisquick helped young brides win the good-natured war with their mothers—in-law! After the wedding, it was "basic training" with Bisquick, ensuring happy hubbys and victory in the dessert arena.

Strawberry Shortcakes

6 servings

2 1/3 cups Original Bisquick

1/2 cup milk

3 tablespoons sugar

3 tablespoons margarine or butter, melted

1 quart (4 cups) strawberries, sliced

1 cup Sweetened Whipped Cream (page 195)

1. Heat oven to 425°. Mix Bisquick, milk, sugar and margarine until soft dough forms.

2. Drop dough by 6 spoonfuls onto ungreased cookie sheet.

3. Bake 10 to 12 minutes or until golden brown. Split warm shortcakes. Fill and top with strawberries and whipped cream.

High Altitude (3500 to 6500 feet): Heat oven to 450°. Use 1 tablespoon sugar.
1 Serving: Calories 350 (Calories from Fat 160); Fat 18g (Saturated 6g); Cholesterol 20mg; Sodium 760mg; Carbohydrate 45g (Dietary Fiber 3g); Protein 5g. **% Daily Value:** Vitamin A 12%; Vitamin C 90%; Calcium 12%; Iron 10%. **Diet Exchanges:** 2 Starch, 1 Fruit, 3 Fat.

Rolled Shortcakes: Knead dough 10 times. Roll 1/2 inch thick. Cut with 3-inch round cutter dipped in Bisquick.

Pan Shortcake: Spread dough in ungreased round pan, 8 x 1 1/2 inches, or square pan, 8 x 8 x 2 inches. Bake 15 to 20 minutes.

Shortcakes, the sweet sister to biscuits, are simple to make and simply delicious. Here are some surefire shortcake secrets:

1. Stir it up. Stir the ingredients with a spoon until a soft, slightly sticky dough forms.

2. Drop it. Drop the dough by large spoonfuls onto an ungreased cookie sheet. Shiny aluminum cookie sheets of good quality produce the best shortcakes and keep the bottoms from getting overly browned.

3. Bake 'em, but don't burn 'em. Because shortcakes contain a lot of sugar, they will typically have a dark bottom crust. If your cookie sheet is brown, black or darkened from a buildup of fat, the bottoms of the shortcakes may burn. Reducing the oven temperature to 400° may help. Also, make sure to place the cookie sheet on the center oven rack. That way, the shortcakes will brown evenly on both the top and bottom.

4. Stick to it. If the bottoms stick slightly to the cookie sheet, use a metal spatula to lift the shortcakes easily off the cookie sheet.

* *Why are my shortcakes raw and doughy in the center?*
• Not enough Bisquick or too much liquid.
• Oven too hot.
• Not baked long enough.

* *Why are my shortcakes dry and dark?*
• Oven too hot.
• Baked too long.
• Dark cookie sheet was used.

Banana Split Shortcakes

6 servings

2 cups Original Bisquick

1/3 cup sugar

3 tablespoons baking cocoa

3 tablespoons margarine or butter, melted

1/2 cup milk

1 pint (2 cups) vanilla ice cream

1 package (10 ounces) frozen strawberries in syrup, thawed

2 medium bananas, sliced

1/4 cup chocolate fudge topping, heated

Whipped topping, if desired

Maraschino cherries, if desired

1. Heat oven to 425°. Mix Bisquick, sugar and cocoa in medium bowl. Stir in margarine and milk until soft dough forms.

2. Drop dough by 6 spoonfuls onto ungreased cookie sheet.

3. Bake 10 to 12 minutes or until knife inserted in center of shortcake comes out clean. Cool 5 minutes. Split warm shortcakes. Fill with ice cream, strawberries, bananas and fudge topping. Top with whipped topping, cherries and, if desired, additional fudge topping.

High Altitude (3500 to 6500 feet): Heat oven to 450°. Use 2 tablespoons sugar.
1 Serving: Calories 520 (Calories from Fat 180); Fat 20g (Saturated 7g); Cholesterol 25mg; Sodium 720mg; Carbohydrate 81g (Dietary Fiber 3g); Protein 7g. **% Daily Value:** Vitamin A 14%; Vitamin C 40%; Calcium 18%; Iron 12%. **Diet Exchanges:** Not Recommended.

This 1952 ad was a foreshadowing of an even peachier proposition—the World's Largest Peach Shortcake! With four tons of Bisquick and nine tons of peaches, the five-layer shortcake was created in 1981 at the South Carolina Peach Festival. Plenty for even the hungriest spouse!

Banana Split Shortcakes

Quick Fruit Cobbler

6 servings

1 can (21 ounces) fruit pie filling
(any flavor)

1 cup Original Bisquick

1/4 cup milk

1 tablespoon sugar

1 tablespoon margarine or butter,
softened

Whipped topping, if desired

1. Spread pie filling in ungreased 1 1/2-quart casserole.
   Place in cold oven. Heat oven to 400°; let heat
   10 minutes. Remove casserole from oven.

2. While pie filling is heating, stir remaining ingredients
   until soft dough forms. Drop dough by 6 spoonfuls
   onto warm pie filling. Sprinkle with additional sugar
   if desired.

3. Bake 18 to 20 minutes or until topping is golden brown.
   Serve with whipped topping.

High Altitude (3500 to 6500 feet): Bake 16 to 19 minutes.
1 Serving: Calories 200 (Calories from Fat 45); Fat 5g (Saturated 1g); Cholesterol
0mg; Sodium 320mg; Carbohydrate 38g (Dietary Fiber 1g); Protein 2g. **% Daily
Value:** Vitamin A 2%; Vitamin C 0%; Calcium 4%; Iron 4%. **Diet Exchanges:**
1 Starch, 1 1/2 Fruit, 1 Fat.

Betty's Tip For a **Fresh Berry Cobbler,** use 3 cups fresh berries
(blueberries, raspberries, sliced strawberries) instead of the canned
fruit. Add sugar to taste to the berries and about 3/4 cup water.
Continue as directed.

Quick Fruit Cobbler

Peach-Toffee Crisp

6 servings

5 medium peaches (2 pounds),
   peeled and sliced (5 cups) or
   5 cups frozen (thawed) sliced
   peaches

2/3 cup quick-cooking oats

1/2 cup packed brown sugar

1/2 cup Original Bisquick

1/4 cup English toffee bits

1/4 cup firm margarine or butter

1 teaspoon ground cinnamon

1. Heat oven to 375°. Spread peaches in ungreased square pan, 8 x 8 x 2 inches.

2. Mix remaining ingredients until crumbly; sprinkle over peaches.

3. Bake 35 to 40 minutes or until peaches are tender and topping is golden brown. Serve warm.

High Altitude (3500 to 6500 feet): Heat oven to 400°.
1 Serving: Calories 270 (Calories from Fat 90); Fat 10g (Saturated 2g); Cholesterol 0mg; Sodium 280mg; Carbohydrate 45g (Dietary Fiber 3g); Protein 3g. **% Daily Value:** Vitamin A 16%; Vitamin C 4%; Calcium 6%; Iron 6%. **Diet Exchanges:** 1 Starch, 2 Fruit, 2 Fat.

Betty's Tip   For awesome **Apple-Toffee Crisp,** substitute 5 cups sliced peeled all-purpose apples for the peaches.

Peach-Toffee Crisp

All-Time
FAVORITE

Velvet Crumb Cake

8 servings

1 1/2 cups Original Bisquick

1/2 cup sugar

1/2 cup milk or water

2 tablespoons shortening

1 teaspoon vanilla

1 egg

Coconut Topping (below)

1. Heat oven to 350°. Grease and flour square pan, 8 x 8 x 2 inches or round pan, 9 x 1 1/2 inches.

2. Beat all ingredients except Coconut Topping in large bowl with electric mixer on low speed 30 seconds, scraping bowl constantly. Beat on medium speed 4 minutes, scraping bowl occasionally. Pour into pan.

3. Bake 30 to 35 minutes or until toothpick inserted in center comes out clean; cool slightly. Make Coconut Topping; spread over cake. Set oven control to broil. Broil cake with top 3 inches from heat about 3 minutes or until topping is golden brown.

Coconut Topping

1/2 cup flaked coconut

1/3 cup packed brown sugar

1/4 cup chopped nuts

3 tablespoons margarine or butter, softened

2 tablespoons milk

Mix all ingredients.

High Altitude (3500 to 6500 feet): Heat oven to 375°. Use 1 1/3 cups Bisquick. Stir 1/3 cup all-purpose flour into Bisquick. Use 2/3 cup milk in cake. Bake about 25 minutes.
1 Serving: Calories 310 (Calories from Fat 145); Fat 16g (Saturated 4g); Cholesterol 25mg; Sodium 410mg; Carbohydrate 39g (Dietary Fiber 1g); Protein 3g. **% Daily Value:** Vitamin A 8%; Vitamin C 0%; Calcium 8%; Iron 6%. **Diet Exchanges:** Not Recommended.

✳ *Why is my Velvet Crumb Cake dry and crumbly?*
• Too much Bisquick or not enough liquid.
• Oven too hot.
• Baked too long.
• Pan size too large.

✳ *Why is my Velvet Crumb Cake heavy and why didn't it rise?*
• Not enough Bisquick or too much liquid.
• Not baked soon enough after batter poured into pan.
• Oven too cool.
• Not baked long enough.

Caramel-Apple Cake

6 servings

1 1/2 cups Original Bisquick

2/3 cup granulated sugar

1/2 cup milk

2 medium cooking apples, peeled
   and sliced (2 cups)

1 tablespoon lemon juice

3/4 cup packed brown sugar

1/2 teaspoon ground cinnamon

1 cup boiling water

Ice cream or whipped cream,
   if desired

1. Heat oven to 350°. Mix Bisquick and granulated sugar in medium bowl. Stir in milk until blended.

2. Pour batter into ungreased square pan, 9 x 9 x 2 inches. Top with apples; sprinkle with lemon juice. Mix brown sugar and cinnamon; sprinkle over apples. Pour boiling water over apples.

3. Bake 50 to 60 minutes or until toothpick inserted in center comes out clean. Serve warm with ice cream.

High Altitude (3500 to 6500 feet): Not Recommended.
1 Serving: Calories 355 (Calories from Fat 45); Fat 5g (Saturated 1g); Cholesterol 0mg; Sodium 450mg; Carbohydrate 75g (Dietary Fiber 1g); Protein 3g. **% Daily Value:** Vitamin A 0%; Vitamin C 2%; Calcium 10%; Iron 8%. **Diet Exchanges:** Not Recommended.

Betty's Tip For a festive presentation, sprinkle the dish with ground cinnamon or nutmeg.

Caramel-Apple Cake

Cream Cheese Pound Cake

10 servings

3 cups Original Bisquick

1 1/2 cups granulated sugar

3/4 cup margarine or butter, softened

1/2 cup all-purpose flour

1 teaspoon vanilla

1/8 teaspoon salt

6 eggs

1 package (8 ounces) cream cheese, softened

Powdered sugar, if desired

1. Heat oven to 350°. Grease and flour 12-cup bundt cake pan or 2 loaf pans, 9 x 5 x 3 inches.

2. Beat all ingredients except powdered sugar in large bowl with electric mixer on low speed 30 seconds, scraping bowl frequently. Beat on medium speed 4 minutes, scraping bowl occasionally. Pour into pan.

3. Bake 55 to 60 minutes or until toothpick inserted near center comes out clean. Cool 5 minutes. Turn pan upside down onto wire rack or heatproof serving plate; remove pan. Cool cake completely, about 1 hour. Sprinkle with powdered sugar.

High Altitude (3500 to 6500 feet): Heat oven to 375°. Do not use loaf pans. Use 2 1/2 cups Bisquick, 1 1/4 cups granulated sugar and 1 cup flour. Bake 45 to 50 minutes.

1 Serving: Calories 535 (Calories from Fat 270); Fat 30g (Saturated 10g); Cholesterol 150mg; Sodium 830mg; Carbohydrate 58g (Dietary Fiber 1g); Protein 9g. **% Daily Value:** Vitamin A 30%; Vitamin C 0%; Calcium 10%; Iron 10%. **Diet Exchanges:** Not Recommended.

Betty's Tip Leftover cake? Make a **Cream Cheese Trifle:** Cut the cake into large cubes, and place them in a large glass or plastic bowl. Sprinkle with a little orange-flavored liqueur or orange juice, cover with plastic warp and refrigerate about 2 hours. Layer cake, whipped cream and fresh fruit in goblets. Cover and refrigerate at least 1 hour before serving.

Cream Cheese Pound Cake

Rhubarb Meringue Torte

12 servings

1 cup Original Bisquick

1/4 cup margarine or butter, softened

1 tablespoon sugar

3 eggs, separated

1 cup sugar

2 tablespoons Original Bisquick

1/2 cup half-and-half

2 1/2 cups cut-up rhubarb

1/3 cup sugar

2 teaspoons vanilla

1/2 cup chopped walnuts

1. Heat oven to 350°. Stir 1 cup Bisquick, the margarine and 1 tablespoon sugar until dough forms. Press dough evenly in bottom of ungreased springform pan, 9 x 3 inches, using fingers dusted with Bisquick. Bake 10 to 15 minutes or until light golden brown.

2. Mix egg yolks, 1 cup sugar, 2 tablespoons Bisquick and the half-and-half in large bowl. Stir in rhubarb. Pour over hot crust. Bake about 45 minutes or until edge is golden brown.

3. Beat egg whites in medium bowl with electric mixer on high speed until foamy. Beat in 1/3 cup sugar, 1 table-spoon at a time; continue beating until stiff and glossy. Do not underbeat. Beat in vanilla. Spread over rhubarb mixture; sprinkle with walnuts. Bake about 15 minutes or until light brown. Cool 10 minutes. Run knife around edge of torte to loosen; remove side of pan. Serve torte warm or cool. Store covered in refrigerator.

High Altitude (3500 to 6500 feet): Bake crust 18 to 20 minutes in step 1. Use 1/4 cup Bisquick instead of 2 tablespoons. Bake torte about 18 minutes in step 3.
1 Serving: Calories 250 (Calories from Fat 110); Fat 12g (Saturated 5g); Cholesterol 70mg; Sodium 210mg; Carbohydrate 32g (Dietary Fiber 1g); Protein 4g. **% Daily Value:** Vitamin A 6%; Vitamin C 0%; Calcium 8%; Iron 4%. **Diet Exchanges:** 1 Starch, 1 Fruit, 2 Fat.

Betty's Tip When choosing fresh rhubarb, pick the cream of the crop. Stalks will range in color from rosy pink to bright red. Select thin, firm, crisp stalks, and avoid thick or wilted ones. Store rhubarb in the refrigerator, loosely wrapped in plastic wrap, for up to a week. Or slice and freeze it up to six months.

Rhubarb Meringue Torte

Black Bottom Cherry Dessert

8 servings

2/3 cup powdered sugar

1/2 teaspoon almond extract

1 egg

1 package (3 ounces) cream cheese, softened

1 3/4 cups Original Bisquick

2/3 cup miniature semisweet chocolate chips

1 can (21 ounces) cherry pie filling

1/4 cup white baking chips

2 teaspoons shortening

1. Heat oven to 400°. Mix powdered sugar, almond extract, egg and cream cheese in medium bowl. Stir in Bisquick. Roll or pat dough into 12-inch circle on ungreased cookie sheet. Flute edge if desired. Bake 8 to 10 minutes or until crust is light golden brown.

2. Sprinkle chocolate chips over hot crust. Bake about 1 minute or until chips are melted; spread evenly. Cool 5 minutes. Gently loosen and transfer to serving plate.

3. Spread pie filling over chocolate. Heat white baking chips and shortening over low heat, stirring frequently, until smooth; drizzle over pie filling.

High Altitude (3500 to 6500 feet): Lightly grease cookie sheet. Bake crust 9 to 11 minutes in step 1.

1 Serving: Calories 385 (Calories from Fat 145); Fat 16g (Saturated 9g); Cholesterol 40mg; Sodium 420mg; Carbohydrate 58g (Dietary Fiber 2g); Protein 4g. **% Daily Value:** Vitamin A 4%; Vitamin C 2%; Calcium 8%; Iron 8%. **Diet Exchanges:** Not Recommended.

Betty's Tip You'll find that using a fork makes it easy to drizzle the melted white baking chips over the cherry pie filling.

Black Bottom Cherry Dessert

Raspberry Truffle Tart

12 servings

1 1/4 cups Original Bisquick

1/2 cup powdered sugar

1/2 cup finely chopped pecans

1/4 cup firm margarine or butter

1 tablespoon hot water

2/3 cup raspberry preserves, melted

1 cup whipping (heavy) cream

1 bag (12 ounces) semisweet chocolate chips (2 cups)

2 tablespoons raspberry liqueur, if desired

1 pint (2 cups) raspberries

1. Heat oven to 350°. Grease tart pan with removable bottom, about 9 x 1 inch, or springform pan, 9 x 3 inches. Mix Bisquick, powdered sugar and pecans in medium bowl. Cut in margarine, using pastry blender or crisscrossing 2 knives, until mixture is crumbly. Stir in hot water. Press mixture firmly in bottom of tart pan. Bake 15 to 20 minutes or until crust is set but not brown. Brush with 1/3 cup of the preserves. Cool completely.

2. Heat whipping cream and chocolate chips in 1-quart saucepan over medium heat, stirring constantly, until smooth; remove from heat. Stir in liqueur. Pour over crust; spread evenly. Refrigerate at least 2 hours until set.

3. Brush remaining preserves over chocolate layer. Top with raspberries. Refrigerate at least 15 minutes before serving. Remove side of pan. Cut tart into wedges. Store covered in refrigerator.

High Altitude (3500 to 6500 feet): Heat oven to 375°.
1 Serving: Calories 395 (Calories from Fat 215); Fat 24g (Saturated 10g); Cholesterol 20mg; Sodium 250mg; Carbohydrate 46g (Dietary Fiber 4g); Protein 3g. **% Daily Value:** Vitamin A 10%; Vitamin C 12%; Calcium 6%; Iron 8%. **Diet Exchanges:** Not Recommended.

Betty's Tip A sprinkling of powdered sugar on dark plates or a dusting of baking cocoa on a white platter adds an impressive finishing touch to this elegant dessert. For an extra special touch, make sugared mint leaves. Mix small amounts of powdered egg whites and water (or use pasturized egg whites) and paint onto mint leaves that you have washed and patted dry. Sprinkle with sugar. Let stand on wire rack until dry.

Raspberry Truffle Tart

Easy Blueberry Tart

8 servings

2 cups Original Bisquick

1/4 cup sugar

1/4 cup margarine or butter, softened

1 can (21 ounces) blueberry pie filling

1/2 cup dried cranberries

1 teaspoon grated orange peel

1. Heat oven to 375°. Mix Bisquick and sugar in medium bowl. Cut in margarine, using pastry blender or criss-crossing 2 knives, until mixture is crumbly. Press firmly on bottom and up side of ungreased tart pan with removable bottom, about 9 x 1 inch, or springform pan, 9 x 3 inches.

2. Bake 12 to 15 minutes or until light brown; cool slightly. Remove side of pan. Cool crust completely, about 30 minutes.

3. Mix pie filling, cranberries and orange peel; spread evenly over crust. Cut into wedges. Store covered in refrigerator.

High Altitude (3500 to 6500 feet): Bake 18 to 20 minutes.
1 Serving: Calories 280 (Calories from Fat 90); Fat 10g (Saturated 5g); Cholesterol 15mg; Sodium 470mg; Carbohydrate 50g; (Dietary Fiber 4g); Protein 2g. **% Daily Value:** Vitamin A 4%; Vitamin C 16%; Calcium 6%; Iron 6%. **Diet Exchanges:** 1 Starch, 2 Fruit, 2 Fat.

Betty's Tip A tangy hint of citrus gives this easy tart new zest. Opt for orange, or try a little lemon or lime. Use a citrus zester or fine grater to remove the peel from citrus fruit. Be careful to grate only the colorful peel. The white part, or *pith*, is quite bitter.

Easy Blueberry Tart

Kiwi-Berry Tarts
6 servings

1 cup Original Bisquick

2 tablespoons sugar

1 tablespoon margarine or butter, softened

2 packages (3 ounces each) cream cheese, softened

1/4 cup sugar

1/4 cup sour cream

1 1/2 cups assorted berries (raspberries, strawberries, blueberries)

2 kiwifruit, peeled and sliced

1/3 cup apple jelly, melted

1. Heat oven to 375°. Mix Bisquick, 2 tablespoons sugar, the margarine and 1 package cream cheese in small bowl until dough forms a ball.

2. Divide dough into 6 parts. Press dough on bottom and 3/4 inch up side of 6 tart pans, 4 1/4 x 1 inch, or 10-ounce custard cups. Place on cookie sheet. Bake 10 to 12 minutes or until light brown; cool on wire rack. Remove tart shells from pans.

3. Beat remaining package of cream cheese, 1/4 cup sugar and the sour cream with electric mixer on medium speed until smooth. Spoon into tart shells, spreading over bottoms. Top with berries and kiwifruit. Brush with jelly. Store covered in refrigerator.

High Altitude (3500 to 6500 feet): Bake 12 to 14 minutes.
1 Serving: Calories 335 (Calories from fat 155); Fat 17g (Saturated 8g); Cholesterol 35mg; Sodium 410mg; Carbohydrate 44g (Dietary Fiber 3g); Protein 4g. **% Daily Value:** Vitamin A 14%; Vitamin C 64%; Calcium 8%; Iron 6%. **Diet Exchanges:** Not Recommended.

Betty's Tip If you don't have apple jelly on hand, you can use raspberry jelly or seedless raspberry jam instead.

Kiwi-Berry Tarts

Pear-Raisin Pie

8 servings

Streusel Topping (below)

1 cup Original Bisquick

1/4 cup margarine or butter,
    softened

2 tablespoons boiling water

1/2 cup pineapple juice

1/2 cup raisins

1 tablespoon cornstarch

1/8 teaspoon ground nutmeg

1/8 teaspoon ground ginger

3 medium pears, peeled and
    sliced (2 cups)

1. Heat oven to 375°. Make Streusel Topping; set aside. Stir Bisquick and margarine in medium bowl until blended. Add boiling water; stir vigorously until very soft dough forms. Press dough firmly in ungreased pie plate, 9 x 1 1/4 inches, bringing dough onto rim of pie plate. Flute edge if desired.

2. Mix pineapple juice, raisins, cornstarch, nutmeg and ginger in 2-quart saucepan. Cook over medium heat, stirring constantly, until mixture thickens and boils. Boil and stir 1 minute; remove from heat. Stir in pears. Spoon into pie plate. Sprinkle with topping.

3. Bake 25 to 30 minutes or until crust and topping are light golden brown.

Streusel Topping

2/3 cup quick-cooking oats

1/2 cup Original Bisquick

1/3 cup packed brown sugar

1/4 cup firm margarine or butter

Mix oats, Bisquick and brown sugar. Cut in margarine, using fork or pastry blender, until mixture is crumbly.

High Altitude (3500 to 6500 feet): No changes.
1 Serving: Calories 325 (Calories from Fat 135); Fat 15g (Saturated 3g); Cholesterol 0mg; Sodium 480mg; Carbohydrate 47g (Dietary Fiber 3g); Protein 3g. **% Daily Value:** Vitamin A 16%; Vitamin C 4%; Calcium 6%; Iron 8%. **Diet Exchanges:** Not Recommended.

Pear-Raisin Pie

Fluffy Key Lime Pie

8 servings

Pat-in-the-Pan Pie Crust (below)

1 can (14 ounces) sweetened condensed milk

1/2 cup Key lime juice or regular lime juice

1 container (8 ounces) frozen whipped topping, thawed

1 tablespoon grated lime peel

Lime slices, if desired

1. Make Pat-in-the-Pan Pie Crust.
2. Beat milk and lime juice in large bowl with electric mixer on medium speed until smooth and thickened. Fold in whipped topping and lime peel. Spoon into pie crust.
3. Cover and refrigerate about 2 hours or until set. Garnish with lime slices. Store covered in refrigerator.

Pat-in-the-Pan Pie Crust

1 cup Original Bisquick

1/4 cup margarine or butter, softened

2 tablespoons boiling water

Heat oven to 400°. Mix Bisquick and margarine in medium bowl. Add boiling water; stir vigorously until very soft dough forms. Press dough firmly in pie plate, 9 x 1 1/4 inches, bringing dough onto rim of plate, using fingers dusted with Bisquick. Flute edge if desired. Freeze 15 minutes. Bake 8 to 10 minutes or until light golden brown. Cool completely on wire rack, about 30 minutes.

High Altitude (3500 to 6500 feet): Bake crust 10 to 12 minutes.
1 Serving: Calories 355 (Calories from Fat 135); Fat 15g (Saturated 8g); Cholesterol 40mg; Sodium 340mg; Carbohydrate 48g (Dietary Fiber 0g); Protein 7g. **% Daily Value:** Vitamin A 8%; Vitamin C 10%; Calcium 22%; Iron 2%. **Diet Exchanges:** Not Recommended.

Betty's Tip A native Florida fruit, Key limes are smaller, rounder, more yellow in color and more tart than the prevalent green Persian limes. If Key limes aren't available in your grocery store, look for bottled Key lime juice near the other bottled lime juices.

Fluffy Key Lime Pie

Frozen Tiramisu Squares

15 servings

1 cup Original Bisquick

1/2 cup sugar

1/3 cup baking cocoa

1 tablespoon instant espresso coffee (dry)

1/3 cup margarine or butter, melted

2 packages (8 ounces each) cream cheese, softened

1 can (14 ounces) sweetened condensed milk

1/4 cup frozen (thawed) orange juice concentrate

1 teaspoon instant espresso coffee (dry)

1 tablespoon hot water

1/4 cup chocolate-flavored syrup

1 1/2 cups whipping (heavy) cream

Baking cocoa, if desired

1. Heat oven to 350°. Grease rectangular pan, 13 x 9 x 2 inches. Mix Bisquick, sugar, 1/3 cup cocoa, 1 tablespoon coffee and the margarine until crumbly. Crumble mixture lightly into pan. Bake 6 minutes; cool.

2. Beat cream cheese in medium bowl with electric mixer on medium speed until smooth. Gradually beat in milk. Place about 2 cups of the cream cheese mixture in separate bowl. Add juice concentrate to cream cheese mixture in one bowl. Dissolve 1 teaspoon coffee in hot water; stir coffee mixture and chocolate syrup into cream cheese mixture in other bowl. Beat whipping cream in chilled medium bowl on high speed until stiff. Fold half of the whipped cream into each cream cheese mixture. Cover and refrigerate chocolate mixture. Spoon orange mixture over crust.

3. Freeze crust with orange mixture about 1 hour or until firm. Spread chocolate mixture evenly over orange mixture. Freeze about 4 hours or until firm. Let stand 10 minutes at room temperature before serving. For squares, cut into 5 rows by 3 rows. Sprinkle each serving with cocoa. Store covered in freezer.

High Altitude (3500 to 6500 feet): No changes.
1 Serving: Calories 420 (Calories from Fat 245); Fat 27g (Saturated 14g); Cholesterol 70mg; Sodium 320mg; Carbohydrate 38g (Dietary Fiber 1g); Protein 7g. **% Daily Value:** Vitamin A 22%; Vitamin C 12%; Calcium 16%; Iron 6%. **Diet Exchanges:** Not Recommended.

Betty's Tip If you don't have any instant espresso coffee on hand, instant coffee granules will work just fine.

Frozen Tiramisu Squares, Orange-Pecan Biscotti (page 233)

Strawberry Crumble Bars

24 bars

2 cups Original Bisquick

1 cup quick-cooking oats

3/4 cup packed brown sugar

1/2 cup margarine or butter, softened

1 cup strawberry spreadable fruit, jam or preserves

1. Heat oven to 400°. Grease square pan, 9 x 9 x 2 inches. Mix Bisquick, oats and brown sugar in large bowl. Cut in margarine, using fork or pastry blender, until mixture is crumbly.

2. Press half of the crumbly mixture in pan. Spread spreadable fruit over crumbly mixture to within 1/4 inch of edges. Top with remaining crumbly mixture; press gently into fruit.

3. Bake 25 to 30 minutes or until light brown; cool. For bars, cut into 6 rows by 4 rows.

High Altitude (3500 to 6500 feet): Bake 27 to 32 minutes.
1 Bar: Calories 140 (Calories from Fat 45); Fat 5g (Saturated 1g); Cholesterol 0mg; Sodium 200mg; Carbohydrate 24g (Dietary Fiber 1g); Protein 1g. **% Daily Value:** Vitamin A 4%; Vitamin C 0%; Calcium 2%; Iron 4%. **Diet Exchanges:** 1/2 Starch, 1 Fruit, 1 Fat.

Betty's Tip A drizzle of chocolate is an easy way to decorate the tops of these yummy crumble bars. Heat 1/4 cup semisweet chocolate chips and 1/2 teaspoon shortening in the microwave on High 1 to 2 minutes. Stir until completely melted, and drizzle over bars.

Strawberry Crumble Bars

Caramel Turtle Bars

24 bars

1 1/2 cups Original Bisquick

1 cup quick-cooking oats

3/4 cup packed brown sugar

1/3 cup margarine or butter, softened

1 egg

1 bag (14 ounces) caramels

2 tablespoons milk

1 cup chopped pecans

3/4 cup semisweet chocolate chips

1. Heat oven to 350°. Stir Bisquick, oats, brown sugar, margarine and egg until well blended. Press in bottom of ungreased rectangular pan, 13 x 9 x 2 inches. Bake about 15 minutes or until golden brown; cool.

2. Heat caramels and milk in 2-quart saucepan over low heat, stirring frequently, until caramels are melted. Spread over crust. Sprinkle pecans evenly over caramels. Heat chocolate chips over low heat, stirring frequently, until melted. Drizzle over pecans.

3. Cool 30 minutes. For bars, cut into 6 rows by 4 rows.

High Altitude (3500 to 6500 feet): Heat oven to 375°.
1 Bar: Calories 220 (Calories from Fat 90); Fat 10g (Saturated 3g); Cholesterol 10mg; Sodium 190mg; Carbohydrate 31g (Dietary Fiber 1g); Protein 3g. **% Daily Value:** Vitamin A 4%; Vitamin C 0%; Calcium 4%; Iron 4%. **Diet Exchanges:** 1 Starch, 1 Fruit, 2 Fat.

Betty's Tip Think outside the square! To cut triangle shapes, cut squares diagonally in half. To cut diamond shapes, first cut parallel lines 1 or 1 1/2 inches apart down the length of the pan, then cut diagonal lines 1 or 1 1/2 inches apart across the straight cuts. You will find irregularly shaped pieces in the corners at the ends of the pan— consider those extra treats for snacking!

Caramel Turtle Bars, Chocolate Chip Cookies (page 232)

Chocolate Chip Cookies

About 4 1/2 dozen cookies

1/2 cup margarine or butter, softened

1 cup packed brown sugar

2 teaspoons vanilla

1 egg

2 3/4 cups Original Bisquick

1 bag (6 ounces) semisweet chocolate chips (1 cup)

1/2 cup chopped nuts, if desired

1. Heat oven to 375°. Mix margarine, brown sugar, vanilla and egg in large bowl. Stir in Bisquick, chocolate chips and nuts.

2. Drop dough by rounded teaspoonfuls about 2 inches apart onto ungreased cookie sheet; flatten slightly.

3. Bake about 10 minutes or until golden brown. Remove from cookie sheet to wire rack.

High Altitude (3500 to 6500 feet): Heat oven to 400°.
1 Cookie: Calories 80 (Calories from Fat 35); Fat 4g (Saturated 1g); Cholesterol 5mg; Sodium 115mg; Carbohydrate 10g (Dietary Fiber 0g); Protein 1g. **% Daily Value:** Vitamin A 2%; Vitamin C 0%; Calcium 2%; Iron 2%. **Diet Exchanges:** 1/2 Starch, 1 Fat.

Betty's Tip For perfectly shaped cookies, use a small ice-cream scoop to drop cookie dough onto the cookie sheet.

Orange-Pecan Biscotti

About 2 1/2 dozen cookies

1 cup sugar

6 tablespoons margarine or butter, softened

1 tablespoon grated orange peel

2 eggs

3 1/2 cups Original Bisquick

1 cup pecan pieces

1 bag (6 ounces) semisweet chocolate chips (1 cup)

2 teaspoons shortening

1. Heat oven to 350°. Beat sugar, margarine and orange peel in large bowl with electric mixer on medium speed until creamy and well blended. Beat in eggs. Stir in Bisquick and pecans. Place dough on surface sprinkled with Bisquick; gently roll in Bisquick to coat. Shape into a ball; gently knead about 10 times or until dough holds together and pecans are evenly distributed. Divide dough in half. Shape each half into 10 x 3-inch rectangle on ungreased cookie sheet.

2. Bake about 20 minutes or until very light brown. Cool on cookie sheet 15 minutes. Cut each rectangle crosswise into 3/4-inch slices. Turn slices cut sides down on cookie sheet. Bake 10 to 15 minutes or until crisp and light brown. Remove from cookie sheet to wire rack. Cool completely, about 30 minutes.

3. Heat chocolate chips and shortening over low heat, stirring constantly, until chocolate chips are melted. Dip cookies halfway into melted chocolate or drizzle with melted chocolate. Let stand until chocolate is set.

High Altitude (3500 to 6500 feet): Bake about 23 minutes in step 2. Bake 15 to 20 minutes in step 3.

1 Cookie: Calories 150 (Calories from Fat 70); Fat 8g (Saturated 3g); Cholesterol 20mg; Sodium 220mg; Carbohydrate 18g (Dietary Fiber 1g); Protein 2g. **% Daily Value:** Vitamin A 2%; Vitamin C 0%; Calcium 2%; Iron 4%. **Diet Exchanges:** 1 Starch, 1 1/2 Fat.

Betty's Tip For heavenly **Hazelnut Biscotti**, substitute chopped hazelnuts for the pecans and leave out the orange peel. Beat in 1 teaspoon vanilla and 1 teaspoon almond extract with the margarine.

<h1>favorites made
lighter</h1>

Applesauce Gingerbread Cake (page 236), Hearty Chicken and Potato Dinner (page 237)

Applesauce Gingerbread Cake

9 servings

2 1/4 cups Reduced Fat Bisquick

1/3 cup sugar

1/2 cup applesauce

1/2 cup fat-free (skim) milk

1/2 cup molasses

1/4 cup fat-free cholesterol-free egg product, 2 egg whites or 1 egg

1 teaspoon ground cinnamon

1 teaspoon ground ginger

1/4 teaspoon ground cloves

1 cup vanilla fat-free yogurt

1 to 2 tablespoons chopped crystallized ginger

1. Heat oven to 350°. Spray bottom only of square pan, 9 x 9 x 2 inches, with cooking spray.

2. Beat all ingredients except yogurt and crystallized ginger with electric mixer on low speed 30 seconds, scraping bowl constantly. Beat on medium speed 3 minutes, scraping bowl occasionally. Pour into pan.

3. Bake 30 to 35 minutes or until toothpick inserted in center comes out clean. Serve cake warm topped with yogurt and crystallized ginger.

High Altitude (3500 to 6500 feet): Heat oven to 375°. Use 2 1/2 cups Bisquick, 1/4 cup sugar and 2/3 cup milk.

1 Serving: Calories 220 (Calories from Fat 20); Fat 2g (Saturated 1g); Cholesterol 0mg; Sodium 360mg; Carbohydrate 46g (Dietary Fiber 1g); Protein 5g. **% Daily Value:** Vitamin A 4%; Vitamin C 0%; Calcium 12%; Iron 14%. **Diet Exchanges:** 2 Starch, 1 Fruit.

Betty's Tip Crystallized ginger can be a sticky mess to chop. Spray kitchen scissors with a little cooking spray, and snip the ginger into pieces.

Hearty Chicken and Potato Dinner

4 servings

4 boneless, skinless chicken breast halves (about 1 1/4 pounds)

1/4 cup Dijon mustard

3/4 cup Reduced Fat Bisquick

1 1/2 pounds small red potatoes, cut into fourths

1 medium bell pepper, cut into 1/2-inch pieces

1 medium onion, cut into 16 wedges

Cooking spray

1/4 cup grated fat-free Parmesan cheese topping, if desired

1 teaspoon paprika

1. Heat oven to 400°. Spray jelly roll pan, 15 1/2 x 10 1/2 x 1 inch, with cooking spray.

2. Brush chicken with 2 tablespoons of the mustard, then coat with Bisquick. Place 1 chicken breast half in each corner of pan. Place potatoes, bell pepper and onion in center of pan. Brush vegetables with remaining 2 tablespoons mustard. Spray chicken and vegetables with cooking spray. Sprinkle evenly with cheese and paprika.

3. Bake uncovered 35 to 40 minutes, stirring vegetables after 20 minutes, until potatoes are tender and juice of chicken is no longer pink when centers of thickest pieces are cut.

High Altitude (3500 to 6500 feet): Not recommended.
1 Serving: Calories 400 (Calories from Fat 55); Fat 6g (Saturated 2g); Cholesterol 75mg; Sodium 600mg; Carbohydrate 55g (Dietary Fiber 5g); Protein 33g. **% Daily Value:** Vitamin A 18%; Vitamin C 62%; Calcium 7%; Iron 4%. **Diet Exchanges:** 3 Starch, 3 Very Lean Meat, 2 Vegetable.

In the 1930s, Bisquick rides the radio airwaves— flying high with both buyers and advertisers.

Chicken with Garlic-Ginger Sauce

6 servings

1/4 cup fat-free cholesterol-free egg product, 2 egg whites or 1 egg

2 tablespoons water

1 cup Reduced Fat Bisquick

1/4 teaspoon garlic powder

6 small boneless, skinless chicken breast halves (about 1 1/2 pounds)

Cooking spray

4 medium cloves garlic, chopped (2 teaspoons)

1 tablespoon chopped gingerroot

4 medium green onions, chopped (1/4 cup)

1 tablespoon sugar

1 tablespoon soy sauce

1 tablespoon rice vinegar

1 tablespoon cooking sherry, if desired

2 teaspoons toasted sesame oil

1. Heat oven to 425°. Spray jelly roll pan, 15 1/2 x 10 1/2 x 1 inch, with cooking spray. Beat egg product and water slightly. Mix Bisquick and garlic powder. Dip chicken into egg mixture, then coat with Bisquick mixture. Place in pan. Spray chicken with cooking spray.

2. Bake 20 minutes. Turn chicken; spray with cooking spray. Bake about 10 minutes longer or until juice is no longer pink when centers of thickest pieces are cut.

3. Spray 10-inch nonstick skillet with cooking spray; heat over medium-high heat. Cook garlic and gingerroot in skillet 2 minutes, stirring constantly. Add remaining ingredients; cook 1 minute, stirring frequently. Spoon sauce over chicken.

High Altitude (3500 to 6500 feet): No changes.
1 Serving: Calories 220 (Calories from Fat 55); Fat 6g (Saturated 2g); Cholesterol 65mg; Sodium 440mg; Carbohydrate 17g (Dietary Fiber 1g); Protein 26g. **% Daily Value:** Vitamin A 2%; Vitamin C 2%; Calcium 4%; Iron 10%. **Diet Exchanges:** 1 Starch, 3 Very Lean Meat, 1 Fat.

Betty's Tip Enjoy this low-fat favorite with a cool cucumber salad. Top cucumber slices with chopped red onion, a sprinkling of toasted sesame seeds and a splash of red wine vinegar.

Chicken with Garlic-Ginger Sauce

Quick Beef and Salsa Skillet

6 servings

3/4 pound diet-lean or extra-lean ground beef

1 jar (16 ounces) thick-and-chunky salsa

1 can (15 to 16 ounces) kidney beans, undrained

1 can (8 1/2 ounces) whole kernel corn, undrained

1 can (8 ounces) tomato sauce

2 teaspoons chili powder

1 1/2 cups Reduced Fat Bisquick

1/2 cup water

1/3 cup shredded reduced-fat Colby-Monterey Jack cheese (2 ounces), if desired

1. Cook beef in 12-inch skillet over medium heat, stirring occasionally, until brown; drain. Stir in salsa, beans, corn, tomato sauce and 1 teaspoon of the chili powder. Heat to boiling; reduce heat to low.

2. Stir Bisquick, remaining 1 teaspoon chili powder and the water until soft dough forms. Drop by 6 spoonfuls onto simmering beef mixture.

3. Cook uncovered 10 minutes. Cover and cook 8 minutes longer. Sprinkle with cheese. Cover and cook about 2 minutes or until cheese is melted.

High Altitude (3500 to 6500 feet): Cook uncovered 12 minutes in step 3.
1 Serving: Calories 355 (Calories from Fat 90); Fat 10g (Saturated 3g); Cholesterol 35mg; Sodium 1070mg; Carbohydrate 51g (Dietary Fiber 8g); Protein 23g. **% Daily Value:** Vitamin A 12%; Vitamin C 20%; Calcium 8%; Iron 32%. **Diet Exchanges:** 3 Starch, 2 Lean Meat, 1 Vegetable.

Betty's Tip Make an equally delicious and quick meal by substituting ground turkey breast for the ground beef.

Quick Beef and Salsa Skillet

All-Time FAVORITE

Garden Vegetable Bake
6 servings

1 cup chopped zucchini

1 large tomato, chopped (1 cup)

1 medium onion, chopped (1/2 cup)

1/3 cup grated fat-free Parmesan cheese topping

1/2 cup Reduced Fat Bisquick

1 cup fat-free (skim) milk

1/2 cup fat-free cholesterol-free egg product or 2 eggs

1/2 teaspoon salt

1/4 teaspoon pepper

1. Heat oven to 400°. Lightly grease square baking dish, 8 x 8 x 2 inches. Sprinkle zucchini, tomato, onion and cheese in dish.

2. Stir remaining ingredients until blended. Pour over vegetables and cheese.

3. Bake uncovered about 35 minutes or until knife inserted in center comes out clean. Let stand 5 minutes before serving.

High Altitude (3500 to 6500 feet): Use 3/4 cup Bisquick. Bake 35 to 40 minutes.
1 Serving: Calories 85 (Calories from Fat 10); Fat 1g (Saturated 1g); Cholesterol 0mg; Sodium 460mg; Carbohydrate 16g (Dietary Fiber 2g); Protein 5g. **% Daily Value:** Vitamin A 6%; Vitamin C 6%; Calcium 10%; Iron 6%. **Diet Exchanges:** 3 Vegetable.

Betty's Tip For **Chicken Garden Bake,** add 2 cans (5 ounces each) chunk chicken, drained, or 1 cup cut-up cooked chicken with the vegetables.

Garden Vegetable Bake

Southwest Tamale Tart

6 servings

1 cup Reduced Fat Bisquick

1/2 cup cornmeal

1 1/2 cups shredded reduced-fat Cheddar cheese (6 ounces)

1 can (4 ounces) chopped green chilies, drained

1/3 cup condensed beef broth

1 can (15 ounces) black beans, rinsed and drained

1/2 cup chopped fresh cilantro

2 small tomatoes, seeded and chopped

Salsa, if desired

Fat-free sour cream, if desired

1. Heat oven to 350°. Grease springform pan, 9 x 3 inches.

2. Mix Bisquick, cornmeal, 1 cup of the cheese and the chilies. Stir in broth. Pat mixture evenly in bottom of pan. Mix beans and cilantro; spoon over cornmeal mixture to within 1/2 inch of edge. Sprinkle with remaining 1/2 cup cheese.

3. Bake 35 minutes. Loosen side of tart from pan; remove side of pan. Arrange tomatoes around edge of tart. Cut tart into wedges. Serve with salsa and sour cream.

High Altitude (3500 to 6500 feet): Heat oven to 375°. Pat cornmeal mixture evenly in bottom and 1 inch up side of pan. Bake 40 minutes.

1 Serving: Calories 255 (Calories from Fat 35); Fat 4g (Saturated 2g); Cholesterol 5mg; Sodium 770mg; Carbohydrate 44g (Dietary Fiber 6g); Protein 17g. **% Daily Value:** Vitamin A 6%; Vitamin C 16%; Calcium 18%; Iron 18%. **Diet Exchanges:** 2 Starch, 1 Very Lean Meat, 3 Vegetable.

Bisquick lightens up in the '90s with less fat, but keeps the same great taste. Now everyone can say "Yes" to Bisquick!

Southwest Tamale Tart

Very Veggie Pizza Pie

8 servings

1 package (8 ounces) sliced
mushrooms (3 cups)

1 small zucchini, sliced (1 cup)

1 medium bell pepper, sliced

1 clove garlic, finely chopped

2 cups Reduced Fat Bisquick

1/4 cup process cheese sauce or
spread (room temperature)

1/4 cup very hot water

1/2 cup pizza sauce

3/4 cup shredded reduced-fat
mozzarella cheese (3 ounces)

1. Heat oven to 375°. Spray cookie sheet with cooking spray. Spray 10-inch skillet with cooking spray; heat over medium-high heat. Cook mushrooms, zucchini, bell pepper and garlic in skillet about 5 minutes, stirring occasionally, until vegetables are crisp-tender.

2. Stir Bisquick, cheese sauce and hot water until soft dough forms. Place dough on surface sprinkled with Bisquick; roll in Bisquick to coat. Shape into a ball; knead about 5 times or until smooth. Roll or pat dough into 14-inch circle on cookie sheet. Spread pizza sauce over dough to within 3 inches of edge. Top with vegetable mixture. Sprinkle with cheese. Fold edge of dough over mixture.

3. Bake 23 to 25 minutes or until crust is golden brown and cheese is bubbly.

High Altitude (3500 to 6500 feet): Heat oven to 400°. Use 1/3 cup very hot water.
1 Serving: Calories 170 (Calories from Fat 55); Fat 6g (Saturated 2g); Cholesterol 10mg; Sodium 490mg; Carbohydrate 24g (Dietary Fiber 2g); Protein 7g. **% Daily Value:** Vitamin A 4%; Vitamin C 16%; Calcium 12%; Iron 10%. **Diet Exchanges:** 1 Starch, 2 Vegetable, 1 Fat.

Betty's Tip If you prefer a spicier crust, use jalapeño-flavored process cheese sauce or spread.

Very Veggie Pizza Pie

Chocolate-Cinnamon Sundae Cake

9 servings

1 1/3 cups Reduced Fat Bisquick

1/2 cup sugar

1/3 cup baking cocoa

1 teaspoon ground cinnamon

1/4 cup fat-free cholesterol-free egg product, 2 egg whites or 1 egg

2/3 cup fat-free (skim) milk

3 tablespoons margarine or butter, softened

Chocolate-Cinnamon Sauce (below)

1 pint (2 cups) reduced-fat vanilla ice cream, if desired

1. Heat oven to 350°. Grease and flour square pan, 8 x 8 x 2 inches.

2. Beat all ingredients except ice cream and Chocolate-Cinnamon Sauce with electric mixer on low speed 30 seconds, scraping bowl frequently. Beat on medium speed 4 minutes, scraping bowl occasionally. Pour into pan.

3. Bake 30 to 35 minutes or until toothpick inserted in center comes out clean. Drizzle with Chocolate-Cinnamon Sauce. Serve warm or cool topped with ice cream.

Chocolate-Cinnamon Sauce

1 cup chocolate-flavored syrup

1/2 teaspoon ground cinnamon

Heat ingredients in 1-quart saucepan over medium-low heat, stirring occasionally, until warm. Serve warm or cool.

High Altitude (3500 to 6500 feet): No changes.
1 Serving: Calories 240 (Calories from Fat 55); Fat 6g (Saturated 1g); Cholesterol 0mg; Sodium 300mg; Carbohydrate 45g (Dietary Fiber 2g); Protein 4g. **% Daily Value:** Vitamin A 6%; Vitamin C 0%; Calcium 4%; Iron 12%. **Diet Exchanges:** 2 Starch, 1 Fruit, 1/2 Fat.

Betty's Tip For the kid at heart, serve this gooey dessert in a sundae bowl, and top it off with a maraschino cherry.

Chocolate-Cinnamon Sundae Cake

Glazed Lemon Bars

24 bars

1 cup Reduced Fat Bisquick

2 tablespoons powdered sugar

2 tablespoons firm margarine
   or butter

3/4 cup granulated sugar

1/2 cup fat-free cholesterol-free
   egg product, 4 egg whites or
   2 eggs

1 tablespoon Reduced Fat Bisquick

2 teaspoons grated lemon peel

2 tablespoons lemon juice

Lemon Glaze (below)

1. Heat oven to 350°. Mix 1 cup Bisquick and the powdered sugar in small bowl. Cut in margarine, using pastry blender or crisscrossing 2 knives, until mixture looks like fine crumbs. Press mixture in bottom and 1/2 inch up edges of ungreased square pan, 8 x 8 x 2 inches.

2. Bake about 10 minutes or until light brown. Mix remaining ingredients except Lemon Glaze; pour over baked layer.

3. Bake about 25 minutes or until set and golden brown. While warm, loosen edges from sides of pan. Spread with Lemon Glaze. Cool completely, about 1 hour. For bars, cut into 6 rows by 4 rows.

Lemon Glaze

3/4 cup powdered sugar

1 tablespoon plus 1 1/2 teaspoons lemon juice

Stir ingredients until smooth.

High Altitude (3500 to 6500 feet): Use square pan, 9 x 9 x 2 inches. Press crust in bottom only of pan. Increase bake time in step 2 to about 12 minutes.
1 Bar: Calories 70 (Calories from Fat 10); Fat 1g (Saturated 0g); Cholesterol 0mg; Sodium 80mg; Carbohydrate 14g (Dietary Fiber 0g); Protein 1g. **% Daily Value:** Vitamin A 0%; Vitamin C %; Calcium 0%; Iron 0%. **Diet Exchanges:** 1 Starch.

Betty's Tip Here's an easy rule of thumb—one fresh lemon will give you 2 to 3 tablespoons of juice. To get the most juice out of a lemon, it should be at room temperature. Some people like to zap whole lemons in the microwave on High for about 20 seconds or so to warm them.

Glazed Lemon Bars

Peanut Butter Brownies

36 brownies

1 1/2 cups Reduced Fat Bisquick

1 cup sugar

1/2 cup applesauce

1/2 cup chunky peanut butter

1/2 cup fat-free cholesterol-free
egg product, 4 egg whites or
2 eggs

1 1/2 teaspoons vanilla

3 ounces semisweet baking
chocolate, melted and cooled

1. Heat oven to 350°. Stir all ingredients until blended.

2. Spread in ungreased rectangular pan, 13 x 9 x 2 inches.

3. Bake 20 to 25 minutes or until set; cool. For brownies,
cut into 9 rows by 4 rows.

High Altitude (3500 to 6500 feet): Bake 30 to 35 minutes.
1 Brownie: Calories 75 (Calories from Fat 25); Fat 3g (Saturated 1g); Cholesterol
0mg; Sodium 75mg; Carbohydrate 11g (Dietary Fiber 1g); Protein 2g. **% Daily Value:**
Vitamin A 0%; Vitamin C 0%; Calcium 0%; Iron 2%. **Diet Exchanges:** 1 Starch.

Betty's Tip Add an extra peanut butter drizzle to the tops of these
nutty bars. Heat 1/4 cup peanut butter chips and 1/2 teaspoon
shortening in the microwave on High 1 to 2 minutes. Stir until
completely melted, and drizzle over bars.

Peanut Butter Brownies

Granola Pancakes

6 servings (Three 4-inch pancakes each)

2 cups Reduced Fat Bisquick

1 1/2 cups fat-free (skim) milk

1/4 cup fat-free cholesterol-free
   egg product, 2 egg whites or
   1 egg

1/2 cup low-fat granola

Banana slices, if desired

Maple syrup, if desired

1. Heat griddle or skillet; grease if necessary.

2. Stir Bisquick, milk and egg product in medium bowl
   until blended. Stir in granola. Pour batter by a little less
   than 1/4 cupfuls onto hot griddle.

3. Cook until edges are dry. Turn; cook until golden brown.
   Serve with remaining ingredients and, if desired,
   additional granola.

High Altitude (3500 to 6500 feet): No changes.
1 Serving: Calories 200 (Calories from Fat 27); Fat 3g (Saturated 1g); Cholesterol
0mg; Sodium 500mg; Carbohydrate 37g (Dietary Fiber 1g); Protein 7g. **% Daily
Value:** Vitamin A 8%; Vitamin C 0%; Calcium 12%; Iron 10%. **Diet Exchanges:**
2 1/2 Starch, 1/2 Fat.

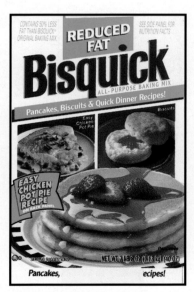

*Bisquick thinks outside the box! This 90s
box shows reduced-fat Bisquick—a great
idea that breaks the mold. How? By offering
terrific taste, with half the fat!*

Granola Pancakes

Berry-Banana Bread

1 loaf (16 slices)

2 cups Reduced Fat Bisquick

3/4 cup quick-cooking oats

2/3 cup sugar

1 cup mashed very ripe bananas (2 medium)

1/2 cup fat-free cholesterol-free egg product, 4 egg whites or 2 eggs

1/4 cup fat-free (skim) milk

1 cup fresh or frozen (rinsed and drained) blueberries

1. Heat oven to 350°. Grease bottom only of loaf pan, 9 x 5 x 3 inches.

2. Stir Bisquick, oats, sugar, bananas, egg product and milk in large bowl until moistened; beat vigorously 30 seconds. Fold in blueberries. Pour into pan.

3. Bake 55 to 60 minutes or until toothpick inserted in center comes out clean. Cool 10 minutes. Loosen sides of loaf from pan; remove from pan to wire rack. Cool completely, about 1 hour, before slicing.

High Altitude (3500 to 6500 feet): Not recommended.
1 Slice: Calories 120 (Calories from Fat 10); Fat 1g (Saturated 0g); Cholesterol 0mg; Sodium 180mg; Carbohydrate 26g (Dietary Fiber 1g); Protein 3g. **% Daily Value:** Vitamin A 0%; Vitamin C 2%; Calcium 2%; Iron 4%. **Diet Exchanges:** 1 Starch, 1/2 Fruit.

Betty's Tip Most quick breads are removed from their pans to a wire rack. This makes a drier, crisper surface. If left in the pan, the bread becomes steamed and soft.

Berry-Banana Bread

Citrus-Yogurt Muffins

12 muffins

1/2 cup fat-free cholesterol-free
   egg product, 4 egg whites or
   2 eggs

2 cups Reduced Fat Bisquick

2/3 cup orange or lemon fat-free
   yogurt

1/3 cup sugar

1/3 cup fat-free (skim) milk

2 tablespoons vegetable oil

1 tablespoon grated orange
   or lemon peel

Orange Glaze (below)

1. Heat oven to 400°. Grease bottoms only of 12 medium muffin cups, 2 1/2 x 1 1/4 inches, or line with paper baking cups.

2. Beat eggs slightly in medium bowl. Stir in remaining ingredients except Orange Glaze just until moistened. Divide batter evenly among cups.

3. Bake 15 to 18 minutes or until golden brown. Cool slightly; remove from pan to wire rack. Drizzle Orange Glaze over warm muffins.

Orange Glaze

1/2 cup powdered sugar

1 tablespoon orange juice

Stir ingredients until smooth.

High Altitude (3500 to 6500 feet): No changes.
1 Muffin: Calories 150 (Calories from Fat 35); Fat 4g (Saturated 1g); Cholesterol 0mg; Sodium 240mg; Carbohydrate 26g (Dietary Fiber 0g); Protein 3g. **% Daily Value:** Vitamin A 2%; Vitamin C 0%; Calcium 4%; Iron 6%. **Diet Exchanges:** 1 Starch, 1 Fruit.

Betty's Tip Mastering the art of muffin making is easy. The key is to not overstir the batter. Mix it just enough to moisten the ingredients, but don't beat it until smooth. Also, make sure to check the muffins at the shortest bake time given in the recipe. Overbaked muffins will be hard and dry.

Citrus-Yogurt Muffins

Cinnamon-Raisin Scone Sticks

10 scone sticks

2 1/2 cups Reduced Fat Bisquick

1/2 cup raisins

1/4 cup plain low-fat yogurt

1/2 cup fat-free (skim) milk

1/2 teaspoon ground cinnamon

1. Heat oven to 450°. Stir all ingredients until soft dough forms. Place dough on surface sprinkled with Bisquick; gently roll in Bisquick to coat. Shape into a ball; knead 5 times.

2. Roll or pat dough into 10 x 6-inch rectangle. Cut crosswise into ten 1-inch strips. Place about 1 inch apart on ungreased cookie sheet.

3. Bake 10 to 12 minutes or until golden brown.

High Altitude (3500 to 6500 feet): No changes.
1 Stick: Calories 135 (Calories from Fat 20); Fat 2g (Saturated 1g); Cholesterol 0mg; Sodium 340mg; Carbohydrate 27g (Dietary Fiber 1g); Protein 3g. **% Daily Value:** Vitamin A 0%; Vitamin C 0%; Calcium 6%; Iron 6%. **Diet Exchanges:** 1 Starch, 1 Fruit.

Betty's Tip These sweet scone sticks are particularly good when eaten warm with a thin spread of honey or jam. Add a glass of fresh-squeezed orange juice, and your morning is off to a sensational start!

Cinnamon-Raisin Scone Sticks

in the kitchen with
kids

Super-Easy Cupcakes (page 264), Sugar Cookie Cutouts (page 265)

Super-Easy Cupcakes

24 cupcakes

3 cups Original Bisquick

1 cup sugar

1/4 cup shortening

1 cup milk or water

2 teaspoons vanilla

2 eggs

1 tub (16 ounces) ready-to-spread
    frosting (any flavor), if desired

1. Heat oven to 375°. Grease and flour 24 medium muffin cups, 2 1/2 x 1 1/4 inches, or line with foil or paper baking cups.

2. Beat all ingredients except frosting in large bowl with electric mixer on low speed 30 seconds, scraping bowl constantly. Beat on medium speed 4 minutes, scraping bowl occasionally. Fill muffin cups about half full.

3. Bake about 15 minutes or until toothpick inserted in center of cupcake comes out clean. Immediately remove from pan to wire rack. Cool completely, about 1 hour. Spread with frosting. Decorate if desired.

High Altitude (3500 to 6500 feet): Heat oven to 400°. Use 3 1/4 cups Bisquick, 3/4 cup sugar and 1 1/4 cups milk or water. Beat on medium speed 2 minutes. Bake about 20 minutes.

1 Cupcake: Calories 125 (Calories from Fat 45); Fat 5g (Saturated 1g); Cholesterol 20mg; Sodium 220mg; Carbohydrate 18g (Dietary Fiber 0g); Protein 2g. **% Daily Value:** Vitamin A 0%; Vitamin C 0%; Calcium 4%; Iron 2%. **Diet Exchanges:** 1 Starch, 1 Fat.

Betty's Tip Kids love cupcakes! To make decorating these kid-friendly treats even easier, freeze the unfrosted baked cupcakes for up to three months. Frozen cupcakes are easier to frost, and you can decorate them any way you like.

Sugar Cookie Cutouts

About 3 dozen cookies

3/4 cup powdered sugar

1/4 cup margarine or butter, softened

1/2 teaspoon almond extract

1 egg

2 cups Original Bisquick

Coarse sugar crystals (decorating sugar), colored glitter sugar, or granulated sugar, if desired

1. Stir all ingredients except Bisquick and granulated sugar in large bowl until well blended. Stir in Bisquick until soft dough forms. Cover and refrigerate 1 to 2 hours or until chilled.

2. Heat oven to 400°. Roll one-fourth of the dough at a time 1/8 inch thick on surface sprinkled with Bisquick. (Keep remaining dough refrigerated until ready to roll.) Cut into desired shapes. Place about 2 inches apart on ungreased cookie sheet. Sprinkle cookies with sugar crystals.

3. Bake 5 to 7 minutes or until edges are light brown. Remove from cookie sheet to wire rack; cool.

High Altitude (3500 to 6500 feet): Use 2/3 cups powdered sugar and 1 3/4 cups Bisquick. Stir 3 tablespoons all-purpose flour into Bisquick. Bake 6 to 8 minutes.
1 Cookie: Calories 55 (Calories from Fat 20); Fat 2g (Saturated 1g); Cholesterol 5mg; Sodium 115mg; Carbohydrate 8g (Dietary Fiber 0g); Protein 1g. **% Daily Value:** Vitamin A 2%; Vitamin C 0%; Calcium 0%; Iron 0%. **Diet Exchanges:** 1/2 Starch, 1/2 Fat.

Betty's Tip Get creative and make some cookie art! Use decorating gels or ready-to-spread frosting, and sprinkle with assorted candy decorations.

Chocolate Kiss–Peanut Butter Cookies

About 3 dozen cookies

1 can (14 ounces) sweetened
  condensed milk

3/4 cup peanut butter

2 cups Original Bisquick

1 teaspoon vanilla

Sugar

About 36 foil-wrapped milk chocolate kisses or milk chocolate
  kisses with white chocolate
  stripes, unwrapped

1. Heat oven to 375°. Stir milk and peanut butter in large bowl until smooth. Stir in Bisquick and vanilla.

2. Shape dough into 1 1/4-inch balls. Roll in sugar. Place 2 inches apart on ungreased cookie sheet.

3. Bake 8 to 10 minutes or until bottoms of cookies just begin to brown. Immediately press chocolate kiss into top of each cookie. Remove from cookie sheet to wire rack; cool.

High Altitude (3500 to 6500 feet): Bake 9 to 11 minutes.
1 Cookie: Calories 130 (Calories from Fat 55); Fat 6g (Saturated 3g); Cholesterol 5mg; Sodium 140mg; Carbohydrate 17g; (Dietary Fiber 0g); Protein 3g. **% Daily Value:** Vitamin A 0%; Vitamin C 0%; Calcium 6%; Iron 2%. **Diet Exchanges:** 1 Starch, 1 Fat.

The '50s really were fabulous with Betty Crocker's 3-step Bisquick cookies!

Chocolate Kiss–Peanut Butter Cookies

Rocky Road Bars

32 bars

1 bag (6 ounces) semisweet
  chocolate chips (1 cup)

2 tablespoons margarine or butter

2 cups Original Bisquick

1 cup sugar

1/2 teaspoon vanilla

2 eggs

1 cup miniature marshmallows

1/4 cup chopped peanuts

1. Heat oven to 350°. Grease bottom only of rectangular pan, 13 x 9 x 2 inches. Heat 1/2 cup of the chocolate chips and the margarine in heavy 1-quart saucepan over low heat, stirring frequently, until melted.

2. Stir Bisquick, sugar, vanilla, eggs and chocolate mixture until blended; spread in pan. Bake 15 minutes. Sprinkle with marshmallows, peanuts and remaining 1/2 cup chocolate chips.

3. Bake 10 to 15 minutes or until marshmallows are light brown. Cool completely, about 1 hour. For bars, cut into 8 rows by 4 rows.

High Altitude (3500 to 6500 feet): Use 3/4 cup sugar.
1 Bar: Calories 115 (Calories from Fat 45); Fat 5g (Saturated 2g); Cholesterol 15mg; Sodium 130mg; Carbohydrate 17g (Dietary Fiber 1g); Protein 1g. **% Daily Value:** Vitamin A 2%; Vitamin C 0%; Calcium 2%; Iron 2%. **Diet Exchanges:** 1 Starch, 1 Fat.

Betty's Tip Earn extra brownie points with the little ones in your family with these bumpy bars of marshmallows, nuts and chocolate. If you're not too nutty about nuts, leave them out and add 1/4 cup white baking chips.

Rocky Road Bars

Banana S'mores

9 servings

3/4 cup graham cracker crumbs

1/2 cup Original Bisquick

2 tablespoons sugar

1/4 cup margarine or butter, melted

2 medium bananas

2 tablespoons lemon juice

1 1/3 cups milk

1 package (4-serving size) vanilla or chocolate instant pudding and pie filling mix

3/4 cup miniature marshmallows

1/2 cup miniature semisweet chocolate chips

1. Mix cracker crumbs, Bisquick and sugar in small bowl. Stir in margarine until moistened. Press in bottom of ungreased square microwavable dish, 8 x 8 x 2 inches. Microwave uncovered on High 1 minute 30 seconds to 3 minutes, rotating dish 1/2 turn every minute, until crust bubbles up slightly and then begins to flatten. Cool 10 minutes on wire rack.

2. Peel and slice bananas; dip into lemon juice. Arrange on cooled crust.

3. Beat milk and pudding mix (dry) with wire whisk or electric mixer on low speed until smooth. Stir in marshmallows. Spread over bananas. Sprinkle with chocolate chips. Refrigerate up to 1 hour before serving. Refrigerate any remaining s'mores.

High Altitude (3500 to 6500 feet): No changes.
1 Serving: Calories 350 (Calories from Fat 110); Fat 12g (Saturated 9g); Cholesterol 25mg; Sodium 520mg; Carbohydrate 59g (Dietary Fiber 2g); Protein 4g. **% Daily Value:** Vitamin A 8%; Vitamin C 8%; Calcium 10%; Iron 6%. **Diet Exchanges:** 1 Starch, 3 Fruit, 2 Fat.

Betty's Tip For a frozen s'mores treat, place the pan of bars in the freezer overnight. Let stand at room temperature for 10 minutes before cutting and serving.

Banana S'mores

Personalized Peanut Butter Pancakes

5 Servings (Three 4-inch pancakes each)

Peanut Butter-Maple Syrup
  (below), if desired

2 cups Original Bisquick

1 3/4 cups milk

1/2 cup creamy peanut butter

2 eggs

1. Make Peanut Butter-Maple Syrup; keep warm. Heat griddle or skillet; grease if necessary.

2. Stir Bisquick, milk, peanut butter and eggs until blended. Pour about 1/2 cup batter into plastic squeeze bottle with narrow opening. Squeeze batter from bottle onto hot griddle to form a letter. (Make letters backward so they will appear "right" when pancakes are served.)

3. When bottom side of letter is brown, pour 1/4 cup batter in circular motion over letter to form pancake. Cook until edges are dry. Turn; cook until golden brown. Serve with syrup.

Peanut Butter-Maple Syrup

1 cup maple-flavored syrup

3 tablespoons creamy peanut butter

Heat ingredients to boiling over medium heat, stirring frequently. Boil and stir 3 minutes.

High Altitude (3500 to 6500 feet): No changes.
1 Serving: Calories 675 (Calories from Fat 260); Fat 29g (Saturated 7g); Cholesterol 90mg; Sodium 990mg; Carbohydrate 88g; (Dietary Fiber 3g); Protein 18g. **% Daily Value:** Vitamin A 6%; Vitamin C 0%; Calcium 20%; Iron 12%. **Diet Exchanges:** 6 Starch, 5 Fat.

The Bisquick box puts a smile on the face of 1960s kids—and anyone else who's young at heart!

Personalized Peanut Butter Pancakes

Jack-O'-Lantern Pizza

8 servings

1 pound ground beef

1 cup salsa

3/4 cup frozen whole kernel corn

1/4 cup water

2 cups Original Bisquick

1/3 cup very hot water

1 tablespoon vegetable oil

2 cups shredded Colby-Monterey
   Jack or Cheddar cheese
   (8 ounces)

Toppings (orange and green bell
   pepper strips, sliced ripe olives,
   chopped red onion, cherry
   tomato wedges), if desired

1. Heat oven to 450°. Grease 12-inch pizza pan. Cook beef in 10-inch skillet over medium heat 8 to 10 minutes, stirring occasionally, until brown; drain. Stir in salsa, corn and 1/4 cup water. Heat to boiling; remove from heat.

2. Stir Bisquick, 1/3 cup hot water and the oil until dough forms; beat vigorously 20 strokes. Let stand 5 minutes. Press dough in pizza pan, using fingers dusted with Bisquick; pinch edge to form 1/2-inch rim. Spread beef mixture over dough. Sprinkle with cheese.

3. Bake 11 to 15 minutes or until crust is golden brown and cheese is melted. Arrange Toppings on pizza to form jack-o'-lanterns.

High Altitude (3500 to 6500 feet): Bake about 15 minutes.
1 Serving: Calories 375 (Calories from Fat 205); Fat 23g (Saturated 10g); Cholesterol 60mg; Sodium 710mg; Carbohydrate 23g (Dietary Fiber 1g); Protein 20g. **% Daily Value:** Vitamin A 10%; Vitamin C 6%; Calcium 24%; Iron 12%. **Diet Exchanges:** 1 1/2 Starch, 2 Medium-Fat Meat, 2 Fat.

It's so easy, it's scary! A 1999 Betty Crocker supermarket magazine recipe uses Bisquick to take the worry out of Halloween, and puts back the fun.

Jack-O'-Lantern Pizza

Pizza Pancakes

5 servings (Three 4-inch pancakes each)

2 cups Original Bisquick

1 cup milk

2 eggs

1/2 cup shredded mozzarella cheese (2 ounces)

1/2 cup chopped pepperoni

1/2 cup chopped tomato

1/4 cup chopped green bell pepper

2 teaspoons Italian seasoning

Pizza or spaghetti sauce, heated, if desired

Grated Parmesan cheese, if desired

1. Heat griddle or skillet; grease if necessary.

2. Stir Bisquick, milk and eggs in large bowl until blended. Stir in remaining ingredients except pizza sauce and Parmesan cheese (batter will be thick). Pour batter by a little less than 1/4 cupfuls onto hot griddle; spread slightly.

3. Cook until edges are dry. Turn; cook until golden brown. Serve topped with pizza sauce and additional pepperoni, tomato and bell pepper. Sprinkle with Parmesan cheese.

High Altitude (3500 to 6500 feet): Spread batter more than slightly on hot griddle. Cook about 2 minutes on each side.

1 Serving: Calories 335 (Calories from fat 155); Fat 17g (Saturated 6g); Cholesterol 105mg; Sodium 1030mg; Carbohydrate 34g (Dietary Fiber 1g); Protein 13g. **% Daily Value:** Vitamin A 8%; Vitamin C 8%; Calcium 24%; Iron 12%. **Diet Exchanges:** 2 Starch, 1 Medium-Fat Meat, 1 Fat.

Betty's Tip Tired of pepperoni? Use chopped smoked turkey or turkey ham instead.

Pizza Pancakes

Hot Dogs 'n' Crescents

8 crescents

1 3/4 cups Original Bisquick

1/3 cup milk

1 tablespoon yellow mustard

3 tablespoons pickle relish, drained

2 slices process American cheese,
  each cut into 4 strips

8 hot dogs

1. Heat oven to 425°. Grease cookie sheet. Stir Bisquick, milk and mustard until soft dough forms; beat 30 seconds. Place dough on surface sprinkled with Bisquick; roll in Bisquick to coat. Shape into a ball; knead 10 times.

2. Roll or pat dough into 13-inch circle; cut into 8 wedges. Place about 1 teaspoon pickle relish and 1 cheese strip on each wedge about 1 inch from rounded edge. Top with hot dog. Roll up, beginning at rounded edge. Place crescents, with tips underneath, on cookie sheet.

3. Bake about 12 minutes or until golden brown.

High Altitude (3500 to 6500 feet): Heat oven to 450°.
1 Crescent: Calories 275 (Calories from Fat 160); Fat 18g (Saturated 7g); Cholesterol 30mg; Sodium 1040mg; Carbohydrate 20g (Dietary Fiber 0g); Protein 8g. **% Daily Value:** Vitamin A 2%; Vitamin C 0%; Calcium 8%; Iron 6%. **Diet Exchanges:** 1 Starch, 1 High-Fat Meat, 2 Fat.

Betty's Tip This is a favorite for kids of all ages. If you like, serve with ketchup and extra mustard for dipping.

Hot Dogs 'n' Crescents

Nacho Pinwheels

6 servings (3 pinwheels each)

3 cups Original Bisquick

3/4 teaspoon chili powder

1/2 teaspoon dried oregano leaves

2/3 cup water

2 tablespoons margarine or butter, melted

1 cup shredded Cheddar cheese (4 ounces)

Salsa, if desired

Sour cream, if desired

1. Heat oven to 425°. Grease cookie sheet. Stir Bisquick, chili powder, oregano and water until soft dough forms. Place dough on surface sprinkled with Bisquick; gently roll in Bisquick to coat. Shape into a ball; knead 10 times.

2. Roll dough into 18 x 10-inch rectangle. Brush margarine over dough. Sprinkle with cheese. Roll up rectangle tightly, beginning at 18-inch side. Pinch edge into roll to seal. Cut into 18 slices. Place on cookie sheet.

3. Bake 11 to 13 minutes or until golden brown. Serve with salsa and sour cream.

High Altitude (3500 to 6500 feet): No changes.
1 Serving: Calories 340 (Calories from Fat 160); Fat 18g (Saturated 7g); Cholesterol 20mg; Sodium 1020mg; Carbohydrate 37g (Dietary Fiber 1g); Protein 9g. **% Daily Value:** Vitamin A 10%; Vitamin C 0%; Calcium 20%; Iron 10%. **Diet Exchanges:** 2 1/2 Starch, 3 Fat.

It's all housed in one can't-resist box! This clever 1960 Bisquick box becomes a house for the kids and a world of easy eating for mom and dad.

Nacho Pinwheels

Squeeze and Squiggle Paint

Remember, this paint is to play with, not to eat!

1/3 cup Original Bisquick

1/4 cup salt

1/4 cup water

2 tablespoons tempera powder (any color)

Glitter, if desired

1. Stir Bisquick, salt, water and tempera powder until blended. Pour paint into plastic squeeze bottle with narrow opening. Repeat with different tempera powders to make more colors if desired.

2. Squeeze out designs onto paper or cardboard.

3. Immediately sprinkle glitter over paint. Let dry. Store paint in covered container at room temperature up to 5 days. Stir before using.

High Altitude (3500 to 6500 feet): No changes.

Betty's Tip Don't throw away those plastic squeeze bottles from ketchup and mustard. They make perfect "squeeze-able" paint bottles.

Squeeze and Squiggle Paint

Easy Fun Dough

Remember, this dough is to play with, not to eat!

1 1/4 cups Original Bisquick

1/4 cup salt

1 teaspoon cream of tartar

1 cup water

1 teaspoon food color

1. Mix Bisquick, salt and cream of tartar in 4-cup microwavable measuring cup. Mix water and food color. Stir colored water into dry mixture, a little at a time, until all liquid is added.

2. Microwave uncovered on High 1 minute. Scrape mixture from side of cup and stir. Microwave uncovered 2 to 3 minutes longer, stirring every minute, until mixture almost forms a ball. Let dough stand uncovered about 3 minutes.

3. Place dough on surface sprinkled with Bisquick. Shape into a ball; knead about 1 minute or until smooth. (If dough is sticky, add 1 to 2 tablespoons Bisquick.) Cool 15 minutes. Use dough to make shapes and designs. Store dough in tightly covered container in refrigerator.

Easy Fun Dough can also be baked like cookie dough to make holiday ornaments. Just follow these directions:

1. Heat oven to 225°. After kneading and cooling dough, roll dough about 1/8 inch thick on surface sprinkled with Bisquick. Cut out desired shapes with cookie cutters. Or instead of rolling dough, shape dough into desired shapes. Make a hole in top of each ornament using end of plastic straw. Place on ungreased cookie sheet.

2. Bake 1 hour. Turn ornaments over. Bake 1 to 1 1/2 hours longer or until ornaments sound brittle when tapped.

3. Remove ornaments from cookie sheet with spatula to wire rack. Cool completely, about 1 hour. Tie ribbon or yarn through hole.

High Altitude (3500 to 6500 feet): No changes.

Betty's Tip To make fun designs and shapes, try using different gadgets, such as pinking shears, cookie cutters, garlic press and pizza roller.

Easy Fun Dough

helpful nutrition
and cooking information

Nutrition Guidelines

We provide nutrition information for each recipe that includes calories, fat, cholesterol, sodium, carbohydrate, fiber and protein. Individual food choices can be based on this information

Recommended intake for a daily diet of 2,000 calories as set by the Food and Drug Administration.

Total Fat	Less than 65g
Saturated Fat	Less than 20g
Cholesterol	Less than 300mg
Sodium	Less than 2,400mg
Total Carbohydrate	300g
Dietary Fiber	25g

Criteria Used for Calculating Nutrition Information

■ The first ingredient was used wherever a choice is given (such as 1/3 cup sour cream or plain yogurt).

■ The first ingredient amount was used wherever a range is given (such as 3 to 3 1/2 pound cut-up broiler-fryer chicken).

■ The first serving number was used wherever a range is given (such as 4 to 6 servings).

■ "If desired" ingredients (such as sprinkle with brown sugar if desired) and recipe variations were not included.

■ Only the amount of a marinade or frying oil that is estimated to be absorbed by the food during preparation or cooking was calculated.

Ingredients Used in Recipe Testing and Nutrition Calculations

- Ingredients used for testing represent those that the majority of consumers use in their homes: large eggs, 2% milk, 80% lean ground beef, canned ready-to-use chicken broth, and vegetable oil spread containing not less than 65% fat.

- Fat-free, low-fat or low-sodium products are not used, unless otherwise indicated.

- Solid vegetable shortening (not butter, margarine, cooking sprays or vegetable oil spread as they can cause sticking problems) is used to grease pans, unless otherwise indicated.

Equipment Used in Recipe Testing

We use equipment for testing that the majority of consumers use in their homes. If a specific piece of equipment (such as a wire whisk) is necessary for recipe success, it will be listed in the recipe.

- Cookware and bakeware without nonstick coatings were used, unless otherwise indicated.

- No dark colored, black or insulated bakeware was used.

- When a baking pan is specified in a recipe, a metal pan was used; a baking dish or pie plate means oven-proof glass was used.

- An electric hand mixer was used for mixing only when mixer speeds are specified in the recipe directions. When a mixer speed is not given, a spoon or fork was used.

Cooking Terms Glossary

Beat: Mix ingredients vigorously with spoon, fork, wire whisk, hand beater or electric mixer until smooth and uniform.

Boil: Heat liquid until bubbles rise continuously and break on the surface and steam is given off. For rolling boil, the bubbles form rapidly.

Chop: Cut into coarse or fine irregular pieces with a knife, food chopper, blender or food processor.

Cube: Cut into squares 1/2 inch or larger.

Dice: Cut into squares smaller than 1/2 inch.

Grate: Cut into tiny particles using small rough holes of grater (citrus peel or chocolate).

Grease: Rub the inside surface of a pan with shortening, using pastry brush, piece of waxed paper or paper towel, to prevent food from sticking during baking (as for some casseroles).

Julienne: Cut into thin, matchlike strips, using knife or food processor (vegetables, fruits, meats).

Mix: Combine ingredients in any way that distributes them evenly.

Sauté: Cook foods in hot oil or margarine over medium-high heat with frequent tossing and turning motion.

Shred: Cut into long thin pieces by rubbing food across the holes of a shredder, as for cheese, or by using a knife to slice very thinly, as for cabbage.

Simmer: Cook in liquid just below the boiling point on top of the stove; usually after reducing heat from a boil. Bubbles will rise slowly and break just below the surface.

Stir: Mix ingredients until uniform consistency. Stir once in a while for stirring occasionally, often for stirring frequently and continuously for stirring constantly.

Toss: Tumble ingredients lightly with a lifting motion (such as green salad), usually to coat evenly or mix with another food.

Metric Conversion Guide

Volume

U.S. Units	Canadian Metric	Australian Metric
1/4 teaspoon	1 mL	1 ml
1/2 teaspoon	2 mL	2 ml
1 teaspoon	5 mL	5 ml
1 tablespoon	15 mL	20 ml
1/4 cup	50 mL	60 ml
1/3 cup	75 mL	80 ml
1/2 cup	125 mL	125 ml
2/3 cup	150 mL	170 ml
3/4 cup	175 mL	190 ml
1 cup	250 mL	250 ml
1 quart	1 liter	1 liter
1 1/2 quarts	1.5 liters	1.5 liters
2 quarts	2 liters	2 liters
2 1/2 quarts	2.5 liters	2.5 liters
3 quarts	3 liters	3 liters
4 quarts	4 liters	4 liters

Weight

U.S. Units	Canadian Metric	Australian Metric
1 ounce	30 grams	30 grams
2 ounces	55 grams	60 grams
3 ounces	85 grams	90 grams
4 ounces (1/4 pound)	115 grams	125 grams
8 ounces (1/2 pound)	225 grams	225 grams
16 ounces (1 pound)	455 grams	500 grams
1 pound	455 grams	1/2 kilogram

Note: The recipes in this cookbook have not been developed or tested using metric measures. When converting recipes to metric, some variations in quality may be noted.

Measurements

Inches	Centimeters
1	2.5
2	5.0
3	7.5
4	10.0
5	12.5
6	15.0
7	17.5
8	20.5
9	23.0
10	25.5
11	28.0
12	30.5
13	33.0

Temperatures

Fahrenheit	Celsius
32°	0°
212°	100°
250°	120°
275°	140°
300°	150°
325°	160°
350°	180°
375°	190°
400°	200°
425°	220°
450°	230°
475°	240°
500°	260°

Index

B

Bacon
  in Hawaiian Brunch Pizza, 64, *65*
  in Maple Breakfast Sandwiches, 58, *59*
  quiche, cheesy, 66, *67*
  in Savory Apple Brunch Bake, 62, *63*
  in Stuffed-Crust Pizza, *104*, 106
  in Turkey Club Squares, 142, *143*
Bake
  chicken garden, 242
  do-ahead egg and sausage, 60, *61*
  garden vegetable, 242, *243*
  savory apple brunch, 62, *63*
Baking cocoa
  Banana Split Shortcake, 198, *199*
  Cake, 248, *249*
  Chocolate-Cinnamon Sundae
  Chocolate Waffles with Caramel-Banana Topping, 20, *21*
Balls, sausage-cheese, 68, 77
Bamboo shoots, in Asian Oven Pancake, 156, *157*
Banana(s)
  berry-, bread, 256, *257*
  brown, tip for, 190
  caramel- topping, chocolate waffles with, 20, *21*
  custard pie, impossibly easy, 190, *191*
  -Nut Bread, 44, *45*
  S'mores, 270, *271*
  Split Shortcakes, 198, *199*
  Upside-down Cake, 206
Barbecued Turkey Bake, 140, *141*
Bars
  caramel turtle, 230, *231*
  crumble, strawberry, 228, *229*
  lemon, glazed, 250, *251*
  Peanut Butter Brownies, 252, *253*
  rocky road, 268, *269*
  shaping tips, 230

Basil pesto appetizer squares, 84, *85*
Bean(s)
  black, in Southwest Tamale Tart, 244, *245*
  cannellini, in Tuscan Chicken Torta, 136, *137*
  cannellini, tip about, 136
  great northern, in Southwestern Bean Bake, 152, *153*
  kidney
    Quick Beef and Salsa Skillet, 240, *241*
    Southwestern Bean Bake, 152, *153*
Beef
  Beef Stroganoff Casserole, 114, *115*
  Chili with Corn Dumplings, 108, *109*
  cutting tips, 116
  dumplings, steamed, 76, *79*
  Family-Favorite Stew, *104*, 107
  Impossibly Easy Lasagna Pie, 164, *165*
  Impossibly Easy Taco Pie, *160*, 163
  Italian Sausage Pot Pies, 122, *123*
  Jack-O'-Lantern Pizza, 274, *275*
  Quick Cheeseburger Bake, 112, *113*
  roast, and swiss sandwich bake, 118, *119*
  and salsa skillet, quick, 240, *241*
  Sloppy Joe Bake, 110, *111*
  Steak Bake, 116, *117*
Beer-Battered Onion Rings with Cajun Dipping Sauce, 92, *93*
Belgian Waffles with Berry Cream, 22, *23*
Berry
  -Banana Bread, 256, *257*
  cobbler, fresh, 200
  cream, Belgian waffles with, 22, *23*
  kiwi-, tarts, 220, *221*
Biscotti
  hazelnut, 233
  orange-pecan, 233

Biscuits, 94–95, *95*
  cheese-garlic, *68*, 70
  sage, hot turkey salad with, 146, *147*
  strawberry–cream cheese, 57, *67*
  tips about, 95
Bisquick
  history of, 8–10
  humidity and, 11
  measuring tips, 11
  Reduced Fat versus Original, 11
  storing tips, 11
Bisquick art from archives
  1930s, 237
  1931, 10
  1933, 90
  1936, 10
  1937, 9
  1938, 98
  1940s, 120
  1940, 15
  1943, 10
  1950s, 206, 266
  1952, 38, 198
  1953, 44
  1957, 9, 84
  1959, 9
  1960s, 170, 272
  1960, 280
  1974, 26
  1975, 8
  1980s, 154, 164
  1981, 188
  1986, 8
  1988, 50
  1990s, 110, 244, 254
  1994, 8
  1996, 134
  1999, 70, 274
Bisquick Basics
  Biscuits, 94–95, *95*
  Blueberry Muffins, 48–49, *49*
  Chicken and Dumplings, 132–33, *133*
  Strawberry Shortcakes, 196–97, *197*
  Velvet Crumb Cake, 204–5, *205*
  Waffles, 94–95, *95*
Bites, zucchini, 90, *91*

Cream
  berry, Belgian waffles with,
    22, 23
  lemon filling, 30
  sour
    Hawaiian Brunch Pizza,
      64, *65*
    Mexican Cheese Snacks,
      86, *87*
    topping, for Impossibly Easy
      Cheesecake, 181
  whipped, sweetened, in
    Neapolitan Shortcake Parfaits,
    193, 195
  whipping (heavy), in
    Cherry–Chocolate Chip
      Scones, *47*, 56
    Frozen Tiramisu Squares,
      226, *227*
    Raspberry Truffle Tart,
      216, *217*
    Tropical Macaroon Scones,
      54, *55*
Cream Cheese
  in Black Bottom Cherry Dessert,
    214, *215*
  in Frozen Tiramisu Squares,
    226, *227*
  in Impossibly Easy Cheesecake,
    181, *183*
  in Impossibly Easy Mocha
    Fudge Cheesecake, 182, *183*
  in Kiwi-Berry Tarts, 220, *221*
  Pound Cake, 210, *211*
  strawberry–, biscuits, 57, *67*
  Truffle, 210
Creamy Tuna Garden Wedges,
  82, *83*
Crescents, hot dogs 'n', 278, *279*
Crisp, peach-toffee, 202, *203*
Crispy Baked Fish with Tropical
  Fruit Salsa, 148, *149*
Crumb cake
  how-to instructions, 204–5
  velvet, 204–5, *205*
Crumble bars, strawberry, 228, *229*
Crumble-Topped Cranberry
  Muffins, 52, *53*

Crust
  pie, pat-in-the-pan, 224
  tip about, 104
Crystallized ginger, tip about, 236
Cucumber salad, tip about, 238
Cupcakes
  frosting tip, 264
  super-easy, *262*, 264
Custard, banana, pie, impossibly
  easy, 190, *191*
Cutouts, sugar cookie, *262*, 265

D

Danish
  easy cherry-almond, 36
  easy drop, 36, *37*
Desserts
  Banana Split Shortcakes, 198, *199*
  Black Bottom Cherry Dessert,
    214, *215*
  Caramel-Apple Cake, 208, *209*
  Caramel Turtle Bars, 230, *231*
  Chocolate Chip Cookies, *231*,
    232
  Chocolate Swirl Cake, *193*, 194
  Cream Cheese Pound Cake,
    210, *211*
  Easy Blueberry Tart, 218, *219*
  Fluffy Key Lime Pie, 224, *225*
  Frozen Tiramisu Squares,
    226, *227*
  Impossibly Easy Banana Custard
    Pie, 190, *191*
  Impossibly Easy Cheesecake,
    181, *183*
  Impossibly Easy Cherry-Almond
    Pie, 186, *187*
  Impossibly Easy Coconut Pie,
    160, 162
  Impossibly Easy French Apple
    Pie, 184, *185*
  Impossibly Easy Mocha Fudge
    Cheesecake, 182, *183*
  Impossibly Easy Peach Pie, 184
  Impossibly Easy Pumpkin-Pecan
    Pie, 188, *189*
  Kiwi-Berry Tarts, 220, *221*

Neapolitan Shortcake Parfaits,
  193, 195
Orange-Pecan Biscotti, *227*, 233
Peach-Toffee Crisp, 202, *203*
Pear-Raisin Pie, 222, *223*
Pineapple Upside-down Cake,
  206, *207*
Quick Fruit Cobbler, 200, *201*
Raspberry Truffle Tart, 216, *217*
Rhubarb Meringue Torte, 212, *213*
Strawberry Crumble Bars, 228, *229*
Strawberry Shortcakes, 196, *197*
Velvet Crumb Cake, 204, *205*
Dinners. *See also* Main dishes
  Asian Oven Pancake, 156, *157*
  Barbecued Turkey Bake, 140, *141*
  Beef Stroganoff Casserole,
    114, *115*
  Breaded Pork Chops, 120, *121*
  Cajun Chicken, 126, *127*
  California Pizza, 138, *139*
  Chicken and Dumplings, 132, *133*
  Chili with Corn Dumplings,
    108, *109*
  Crispy Baked Fish with Tropical
    Fruit Salsa, 148, *149*
  Easy Chicken Pot Pie, 134, *135*
  Extra-Easy Veggie Pizza, 154, *155*
  Family-Favorite Stew, *104*, 107
  Hot Turkey Salad with Sage
    Biscuits, 146, *147*
  Italian Sausage Pot Pies, 122, *123*
  Lemon-Apricot Chicken, 130, *131*
  Oven-Fried Chicken, 124, *125*
  Quick Cheeseburger Bake,
    112, *113*
  Roast Beef and Swiss Sandwich
    Bake, 118, *119*
  Sloppy Joe Bake, 110, *111*
  Southwestern Bean Bake, 152, *153*
  Steak Bake, 116, *117*
  Stuffed-Crust Pizza, *104*, 106
  Thai Chicken with Spicy Peanut
    Sauce, 128, *129*
  Tuna Melt Calzone with Cheddar
    Cheese Sauce, 150, *151*
  Turkey and Corn Bread Stuffing
    Casserole, 144, *145*
  Turkey Club Squares, 142, *143*